FAST FOOD

MORGAN ROSE

CURRENCY PRESS
The performing arts publisher

RED
STITCH

THE
ACTORS'
THEATRE

CURRENT THEATRE SERIES

First published in 2022
by Currency Press Pty Ltd,
PO Box 2287, Strawberry Hills, NSW, 2012, Australia
enquiries@currency.com.au
www.currency.com.au

in association with Red Stitch Theatre, Melbourne

Typeset by Brighton Gray for Currency Press.
Cover shows, from left: Lucy Ansell, Kevin Hofbauer, Sarah Sutherland,
Chi Nguyen; photo by Robert Blackburn.
Cover design by Mathias Johansson.

A catalogue record for this
book is available from the
NATIONAL LIBRARY
OF AUSTRALIA
National Library of Australia

Contents

Currency Press acknowledges the Traditional Owners of the Country on which
we live and work. We pay our respects to all Aboriginal and Torres Strait
Islander Elders, past and present.

'The system is not going to save us; we're going to have to save ourselves.'
David Graeber

'Poetry will always be anti-capitalist because it's waste,
and that's what we love about it.'
Eileen Myles

'Dreaming, after all is a form of planning.'
Gloria Steinem

Fast Food was first performed by Red Stitch Actors' Theatre at the Red Stitch Theatre, St Kilda, on 13 May 2022, with the following cast:

TROY	Kevin Hofbauer
G	Lucy Ansell
RIVER	Chi Nguyen
LEONARD	Casey Filips
ROSEMARY	Ella Caldwell

Director and Production Dramaturg, Bridget Balodis
Set and Costume Designer, Sophie Woodward
Lighting Designer, Giovanna Yate Gonzalez
Sound Designer and Composer, Danni Esposito
Lighting Design Mentor, Katie Sfetkidis
Dramaturgs, Tom Healey and Ella Caldwell
Stage Manager, Rain Okpamen

CHARACTERS

TROY, mid-20s. Manager. Been there six and a half years. Male. BIPOC.

G., 19. Team member. Been there four years. Female. BIPOC.

RIVER, 17. Assistant manager. Been there three years. Can be any gender (change pronouns accordingly). BIPOC.

LEONARD, early 20s. Team member. Been there a year and a half. Male. White.

ROSEMARY, mid-40s. Team member. Been there two weeks. Female. White.

The characters of RADIO, PONY, SOMEONE and COW may be approached however you like: voice recordings or projections, doubled with existing characters, cast as separate actors, etc.

SETTING

Back of house at a burger chain. Clean, corporate, chrome.

NOTES

Passages in bold are fantasies. They take place inside the characters' heads.

There is a lot of silence in this play. Duration is our friend. 'A moment' equates a time of sustained action. It is quite possibly very mundane. A 'pause' is shorter than 'a moment' and may include a shift in action or intention.

A slash / indicates the point of interruption for the line immediately following it.

This play went to press before the end of rehearsals and may differ from the play as performed.

Early morning. The kitchen is dim and empty. Weirdly peaceful.

We sit with this for a while.

Then,

TROY *enters and turns on the lights. He retrieves the till money from the back office, he counts it and fills in a form, then exits to the front of the store.*

A long moment of nothing.

One by one the Team Members come in wearing street clothes. They exit into the staffroom and return in uniform and start the tasks of opening.

G. *is first,*

a long moment,

then RIVER.

Another long moment before,

LEONARD *is the last to enter.*

Now they are all prepping things for the day.

We watch this for a while.

Finally,

RIVER: I brought biscuits.

LEONARD: Aw.

RIVER: Just a way of showing my appreciation.

> *It's a box of Arnott's.*

G.: Appreciation of what?

RIVER: Of like. Your work. Want one?

LEONARD: Sure.

> LEONARD *takes several.* RIVER *winces.*

RIVER: Uh, this is for the next two shifts.

LEONARD: Oh sorry.

> *He puts some back.*

RIVER: G.?

G.: No thanks.

RIVER: I'll put them in the staff room.

> RIVER *exits.*

> *A moment.*

G.: Do you want the shittiest biscuit in all the land in exchange for like your soul?

LEONARD: Yeah, but don't take too many cause I have to ration my shit biscuits for all my shit employees.

G.: And isn't she like ... rich?

LEONARD: I mean, I think she's rich-*ish*.

G.: Like, buy two packs man.

LEONARD: Totally.

G.: I hate those biscuits.

LEONARD: They remind me of my grandmother.

G.: Those biscuits aren't biscuits. I actually pity you and your grandmother.

LEONARD: What your grandmother like bakes her own or—

G.: Yeah. She literally bakes her own.

LEONARD: Right. Okay. Well. You clearly had like a really wholesome normal childhood.

G.: River is just sad, man. She can go eat her biscuits herself alone in her room. You can't buy my friendship with like seven dollars' worth of dry—

> RIVER *enters.* G. *and* LEONARD *shut up quickly.*

> RIVER *hovers for a moment then exits.*

G.: Did she hear us?

LEONARD: No way.

> *Pause.*

G.: I thought you were going to your beach thing today.

LEONARD: Alicia called in sick.

G.: Hm.

> *They work.*

> *A moment.*

> RIVER *returns.*

> *Pause.*

G.: What's she sick with?

LEONARD: Dunno.

RIVER: Who?

LEONARD: Alicia.

RIVER: She accidentally put her hand through a window.

LEONARD: Oh.

Pause.

G.: She put her hand through a window?

RIVER: Yeah.

G.: How?

RIVER: I don't know.

G.: Like she punched a window?

RIVER: Maybe?

G.: Hardcore.

Pause.

LEONARD: Last week she had vertigo.

G.: Vertigo?

RIVER: Yeah.

G.: Does that just mean dizzy?

RIVER: Yes, but I think it's actually—

G.: I basically always have vertigo. I have vertigo right now.

LEONARD: That's called a hangover.

G.: It doesn't count as vertigo if you're hungover?

LEONARD: No.

G.: So I can't go home?

LEONARD: You're here for life.

TROY *enters.*

TROY: Have you turned on the fryer and filled the hopper?

G.: I was just about to start on that.

TROY: G., I'm gonna need you take off that lipstick.

G.: This is my natural lip color.

It's clearly not.

TROY: I mean you look cute and all, but if someone from regional comes in—

G. *wipes off her lipstick with the back of her hand.*

Thanks friend. Love your work.

TROY *writes some things on a clipboard.*

Okay! We have twenty minutes to doors and the production bin wasn't cleaned properly last night!

RIVER: I'll take care of it.

TROY: Love your work. I'm gonna turn on the kiosks.

LEONARD: Good luck.

TROY *exits.*

RIVER: Leonard could you work your magic on the production bin?

LEONARD: My magic?

RIVER: You're just great at cleaning.

LEONARD: Right.

Leonard reluctantly starts on the production bin.

A moment with everyone working.

What the fuck. Somebody spilled like soft drink or something all over this.

They all work. Pause.

It's all sticky. What the fuck.

More working.

Who closed?

RIVER: Alex and Alicia.

A glance between G. *and* LEONARD.

They continue working.

Pause.

RIVER *is looking nervously at* G.

Finally,

I thought it looked good.

G.: What?

RIVER: The—like—lipstick.

G.: Oh. Troy's such a fucking nark.

RIVER: I mean. He's …

She is torn.

... yeah.

RIVER *tries to think of something to say but can't.*

Silence.

They work.

Pause.

Finally. A recovery of sorts:

What did everyone get up to last night?

Long pause.

Did you do anything fun Leonard?

LEONARD: Nope.

Pause.

RIVER: Went straight to bed?

LEONARD: Um. Okay. Well, we were supposed to leave for Mel's aunt's beach house for a couple days but yeah. We didn't. So yeah. Pretty much watched *The Block*, studied for anatomy, and went to bed.

RIVER: Right. Cool.

Pause.

So you must be almost finished with your degree by now.

LEONARD: Nah, I have like a hundred more years.

RIVER: It will all be worth it when you're a doctor.

LEONARD: Nurse.

RIVER: Right ... Well I love nurses!

LEONARD: ... Thanks.

RIVER: Anyway, we're glad you're here with us today instead of at the beach.

LEONARD: Mmm.

LEONARD *continues scrubbing the production bin.*

A moment with everyone working.

Sounds of the ocean. LEONARD *looks up. Closes his eyes. Breathes deep.*

We sit with this for a moment. Then,

RIVER: What about you G.?

G.: What?

RIVER: What did you get up to last night?

G.: I was just home.

    …

    On the computer.

RIVER: Amazing.

> *G. makes eye contact with someone in the audience, a friend of sorts, who's in on the joke. All her fantasies include this friend in some way.*

Was it fun?

G.: It was fine.

RIVER: Are you totally hungover today?

G.: A little.

RIVER: So what do you do?

G.: [*to her audience friend*] **She literally can't take a hint.**
    What do you mean?

RIVER: On the computer, what do you do?

G.: All kinds of stuff.

RIVER: Like what kind of stuff?

G.: **Sims 2.**
    Ummm … last night I played some games.

RIVER: What games?

G.: All kinds. **Just Sims 2.**

RIVER: Amazing. So just all night playing on the computer?

G.: Um. I also had dinner. Went for a walk. Did my laundry.

> *A glance towards her friend, she didn't actually do her laundry.*

RIVER: A walk! Like in the middle of the night?

G.: Yeah.

RIVER: Where?

G.: Just out. Through the cemetery.

RIVER: The cemetery?

G.: Uh-huh.

RIVER: Why?

G.: **So. Annoying.** Cause I'm a vampire.

RIVER: Oh.

RIVER *is puzzled.*

Wait. How does that … Like you mean you were visiting your grave or something? But vampires don't have graves do they because—

G.: **It was a joke.** It was a joke.

RIVER: No, I know, I just was thinking why does a vampire / need to go to—

G.: I'm not really a vampire.

RIVER: Yeah I just didn't understand the reference, because vampires technically never / died so—

G.: The cemetery is a shortcut to the servo and my brother wanted ice cream.

RIVER: Oh.

Cool.

RIVER *actively hates herself.*

G. *is busy hating herself as well.*

G.: **She thinks she's better than me.**

Literally, everyone is extra annoying lately.

She looks around.

All so fucking annoying.

They're all judging me.

I can feel it.

Everyone stares at G.. *She looks at them.*

Fuck you. I know what you're thinking.

[*To audience friend*] They think I'm pathetic because I still live at home. I have no plans. I'm not going anywhere. I'm just a sack of shit that plays Sims 2 for hours and hours and hours every day.

[*To her co-workers*] That is what you're thinking, isn't it? Am I right?

ALL: **yeah/yes/uh-huh** [*etc.*]

G.: **Whatever.**

We don't need them, right? I'm just here for the pay cheque.

RIVER: We still need to unwrap the dressing station and could someone bring up three boxes of ten-to-one patties?

G.: I'll get the patties.

G. *exits to the storeroom.*

RIVER *and* LEONARD *work.*

The ocean waves return. LEONARD *looks out into the distance.*
He speaks to himself, not the audience.

LEONARD: **Everything is fine. Peaceful. I'm at the beach. It's warm.**
But not like too warm. It's the perfect temperature. Yeah …

ROSEMARY *enters a little sweaty and dishevelled.*

ROSEMARY: Hi, sorry I'm late. There were replacement buses.

RIVER: Hi. Um. Okay. We'll just have to mark it on your timesheet.

ROSEMARY: I'm generally a really on time kind of person, this is unlike me.

RIVER: Sorry, I don't know your name.

ROSEMARY: Rosemary. I just started last week.

RIVER: We're a little behind now. The grill still needs to be cleaned.

ROSEMARY: Right, okay.

She moves towards the grill.

LEONARD: Wait.

ROSEMARY: Sorry?

LEONARD: You aren't in uniform.

ROSEMARY: Oh, ha! Of course. I'll be right back, I'm a quick changer.

She exits.

LEONARD: What the fuck? Why is there a new person?

RIVER: Who knows.

LEONARD: That's so fuc—

RIVER: Shhhhh.

TROY *enters.*

TROY: Did someone come in?

LEONARD: New person.

TROY: He's late. What's his name?

LEONARD: Her name. Can't remember.

TROY *looks at the roster.*

TROY: Rosemary. It's Rosemary. Where is she?

LEONARD: Changing clothes.

TROY: Right. [*Pause*] Hey River. River. WHAT SORT OF THINGS
DID YOU GET UP TO LAST NIGHT RIVER?

RIVER: [*nervously*] Hahaha.

LEONARD: What are you doing?

TROY: Oh my god. Oh my god, so River and I had an Upper Leadership and Management Training Session on Sunday and they made us do role plays.

LEONARD: Gross.

TROY: And we had to—okay so it was all about 'making employees feel valued' so we had to like practice giving validation and showing interest in employees 'as people' and they gave us sentence starters and River's was WHAT SORT OF THINGS DID YOU GET UP TO LAST NIGHT?

> RIVER *panics*.

RIVER: I mean it's like a normal question.

TROY: WHAT SORT OF THINGS DID YOU GET UP TO LEONARD?

> **The phrase 'What sort of things did you get up to?' echoes around the space.**

> ROSEMARY *comes back*.

Rosemary! I'm Troy.

> ROSEMARY *is confused*.

ROSEMARY: Yeah.

TROY: I'm a shift manager.

ROSEMARY: Yeah, no I know. You're Troy. We worked a shift together last week.

TROY: Oh. Right. Sorry. You look different or something.

ROSEMARY: Really?

TROY: Your hair or something.

ROSEMARY: I haven't changed my hair in ten years.

But it doesn't matter, I'm gonna clean the grill now.

TROY: Love it.

> *The sound of a text message.*

Was that your phone?

ROSEMARY: Ssshhhit.

Sorry, language.

I forgot to put it on vibrate.

TROY: Yeah, sorry you'll have to put that in your locker.

ROSEMARY: Oh. Sorry. On my first shift Izzy said it wasn't a problem so long as it was on vibrate. I have kids, so, you know …

TROY: Izzy said that?

ROSEMARY: Yeah, I think so.

TROY: She shouldn't have said that.

ROSEMARY: Right, okay, no worries.

Okay, Troy, so this would be just for today, but I have an ebay auction running for an Ooshie that finishes at noon. So …

TROY: Ebay.

ROSEMARY: Yeah, it's for a really rare one and I promise to put the phone in my locker right after it finishes.

TROY: Um. Yeah. No phones. It's policy.

> ROSEMARY *nods.*

Sorry.

ROSEMARY: No worries.

TROY: Love it.

> *Pause.*

> ROSEMARY *exits to put her phone away.* TROY *exits to FOH.*

LEONARD: Did she say Ooshie?

RIVER: Yeah.

LEONARD: Ooshie.

RIVER: It's a toy.

> G. *enters with boxes.*

G.: The deep freeze was a fucking disaster. Someone dropped a box of—

> ROSEMARY *re-enters.*

G.: Oh. Hi.

LEONARD: This is Rosemary.

G.: How's it going?

ROSEMARY: Yeah. Good.

G.: I'm G.

ROSEMARY: What?

G.: G.

ROSEMARY: Yeah. I know. It's Rosemary.

G.: Nice to meet you.

ROSEMARY: No, sorry.

G.: What?

ROSEMARY: Sorry, we worked together a couple days ago.

G.: [*to audience friend*] **Shit.** Sorry. I'm really hungover today so.

ROSEMARY: Fair enough.

> ROSEMARY *picks up a wire brush and a spray bottle filled with clear liquid with the letters MPC written on it in sharpie begins to clean the grill.*

LEONARD: Rosemary. Did you say Ooshie?

ROSEMARY: What?

LEONARD: Did you say Ooshie?

ROSEMARY: Yeah! It was the Blue Spirit Mufasa and I was gonna get it for like seventy-five dollars.

G.: / **What is she saying?**

LEONARD: What is she saying?

RIVER: She's saying Ooshie. It's a toy.

ROSEMARY: Yeah, sorry, it's a toy.

LEONARD: Right.

ROSEMARY: Sorry, I'm speaking seven-year-old. They're just from Woolies, but they're like collectibles now and Connor, my youngest, LOVES them, and it's his birthday next month, and everyone in his class wants the Blue Mufasa.

LEONARD: Right …

RIVER: It's like footy cards but for Gen Z.

G.: Yeeeesss! I had so many footy cards.

RIVER: Me too!

G.: I didn't even like footy.

RIVER: Me neither!

> *Music. They make eye contact. The romance is thick.* **RIVER winks or something.** *The music cuts out.* RIVER *is left staring at* G.

G.: What?

> RIVER *looks away quickly:*

RIVER: I can't find the bread knife.

G.: You're holding it.

RIVER: Oh.

ROSEMARY: When I was little it was ponies.

LEONARD: Ponies?

ROSEMARY: My Little Ponies? All the rich pretty girls had like twenty
    ponies and I had two, literally two, and no-one wanted to eat lunch
    with me. So Connor needs that Mufasa.

LEONARD: Just say you're going to the toilet and go check your phone.
    That's what everyone does. Even Troy.

ROSEMARY: Thanks.

RIVER: Okay. Rosemary. Could you get to the grill, because we don't
    have long till customers.

ROSEMARY: Sure.

They work.

A moment.

Music. RIVER *stares at* G.

RIVER: **So what did you get up to last night?**

G. ***laughs a little, nervous:***

G.: **Oh, I don't know. Nothing really. What did you get up to?**

RIVER: **Just a party.**

G.: **That's cool.**

RIVER: **It was lame.**

G.: **Oh right.**

RIVER: **Yeah.**

> **I only stayed til like eleven p.m. No. Like two a.m. One a.m.**
> **I left at one a.m.**
> **I was bored.**
> **So, do you want to get out of here?**

G.: **What?**

RIVER: **C'mon. Screw this joint. (Now hold my hand, you're holding**
    my hand like—yeah …)

> ***They are holding hands now.***

G.: **We'll get in trouble.**

RIVER: **Who cares?**

G.: **You're bad.**

RIVER: **I know.** Oh no sorry. You have to use. Sorry. You need to use GC not the MPC.

ROSEMARY: What?

RIVER: Oh. It's just. You're using the MPC. And you need to use the GC.

> RIVER *holds up a different spray bottle with blue liquid in it. It has the letters 'GC' written on it.*

See this one is for counter—MPC— and this one is for the grill. GC. It's blue. MPC is clear. I'll show you. You just take it ...

> RIVER *takes the wire brush and demonstrates. She is very skilled at this. She's done it hundreds of times.*

And you wanna spray maybe four or five times, and you want some distance from the grill so you get good coverage, and then you take the wire brush and you scrub—

ROSEMARY: Got it. I think I can take it from here.

> RIVER *hands her the wire brush.*

RIVER: Oh. Okay. Great. Yeah just. Make sure you. Sorry. You have to scrape towards yourself so that it falls into this tray right here and then—

ROSEMARY: Right. I've cleaned a grill before. Thanks hon.

> *The term of endearment weirds* RIVER *out. She hovers, unsure of what to do.* ROSEMARY *looks up.*

I've got it love.

> *This weirds* RIVER *out even more.*

RIVER: Okay. Great.

> **RIVER *stares at* ROSEMARY *in a daze of shame and embarrassment.***
>
> **She slaps herself a few times. She feels much better.**
>
> RIVER *emits an odd garbled moan of pain and relief.*
>
> *Everyone looks towards* RIVER.

Can't get this box open.

ROSEMARY: Need help?

RIVER: No, I'm fine.

>   LEONARD *has a box of tomatoes.*

>   *A moment, everyone works.*

LEONARD: Oh my god. Ha!

>   *Everyone keeps working.*

>   This is amazing.

>   *Everyone keeps working.*

>   This is so fucked up. [*To* G.] What does this look like to you?

>   *He shows her the top of the tomato where the stem used to be.*

G.: An asshole.

LEONARD: Exactly! Thank you! [*Looking down at the tomato*] I wish I
   had my phone to take a photo. Look!

>   *He shows it to* ROSEMARY.

ROSEMARY: Oh wow, it really does look like an asshole.

>   *She gets genuine joy from this.*

RIVER: How are you going Rosemary?

ROSEMARY: Oh. Sorry, what?

RIVER: How are you going with everything? Do you need another task?

ROSEMARY: No I'm fine.

RIVER: When you're done with that can you refill the sauce containers.

ROSEMARY: The sauce containers?

RIVER: These right here? They need to be refilled.

ROSEMARY: Oh okay, yup—

RIVER: After the grill.

ROSEMARY: No problem, hon—

RIVER: Stop.

ROSEMARY: What?

RIVER: Um. No. I mean.

>   Sorry.

>   **RIVER *plunges her hand into the deep fryer and endures the pain.***

>   It's just.
>   Hon.
>   The word 'hon'.

Don't.

Like. Don't.

ROSEMARY: Oh. It's meant to be nice.

RIVER: It's not.

I'm assistant manager.

ROSEMARY: Okay. Sorry.

TROY *enters.*

TROY: Brian is back.

RIVER: Oh no.

TROY: Leonard could you go talk to him?

LEONARD: Why me?

TROY: Cause you did it the past few times and he knows you. He responds to you.

LEONARD: I really don't want to.

G.: Why do we need to talk him?

ROSEMARY: Who's Brian?

RIVER: This homeless guy who keeps setting up his bed outside our door.

G.: He's just sleeping. He's not doing anything bad.

TROY: I hear what you're saying, but I need to open soon.

No-one is on board.

He scares away customers!

G.: He literally doesn't. People need burgers and Brian can't stop them.

TROY: Look it's just how we have to deal with it.

G.: Is it?

TROY: I don't make the rules.

LEONARD: You just follow them.

TROY: Leonard, just go talk to him.

Pause.

LEONARD: Fine.

LEONARD *exits.*

TROY: It's my job. It's my job to follow the rules. I have a boss too, you know.

Also Five-S.K.-three is frozen again. River, it only responds to you.

RIVER: I mean that's not true, but sure.

>   RIVER *and* TROY *exit.*

ROSEMARY: What's Five-S.K.-three?

G.: It's one of the self-serve kiosks.

>   ROSEMARY *is lost.*

Like the self-ordering computer things. Out the front.

ROSEMARY: Oh, right.

G.: They're always fucking up.

ROSEMARY: It's the same at the shops. I hate talking to a bloody machine. If I have the option I always choose a person.

G.: I don't mind them at the shops. Like, it's just easier. To like do it yourself.

ROSEMARY: Oh my god, it takes three times as long, I don't want to weigh my own fruit, I'm not trained for that! And we're next, you know? Pretty soon, the robots will be back here cleaning the grill and then you and I will be out of a job. Like I was hoping to work a cash register but apparently that's no longer an option.

G.: Yeah, all our front of house people got laid off like three months ago right after they installed the kiosks. I actually can't believe you got hired.

ROSEMARY: Oh. Right.

>   The owner of this store is a friend of my ex-husband's.
>   So.

G.: Right.

ROSEMARY: This was. Nowhere else would hire me.

>   Sorry.

G.: Not your fault.

>   **G. *shares a moment with her audience friend.***
>
>   *Pause.*
>
>   *They work.*
>
>   RIVER *returns.*
>
>   LEONARD *returns.*
>
>   *They work.*
>
>   *A moment.*

Ocean waves.

LEONARD: **Everything is fine. Peaceful. I'm at the beach. It's warm, but not too warm. It's the perfect temperature. I … actually, I live here. I have a house. I have a beach house because—**

TROY: Could someone give the floor a dry mop real quick?

LEONARD: Yup.

Everything is fine. Peaceful. I have a beach house. Aunt Maggie has died and left me her beach house … No, someone else. Someone else that I don't know very well has died and left me their beach house. It's a beautiful house. Big and calm and clean. I get up early and go for walks alone on the sand and my brain is soft and floppy. Sometimes I take off all my clothes and wade out into the ocean and float while I think about everything and nothing. I look down at my pale body and watch my pubes wave in water—

RIVER: Leonard, sorry, could you set Rosemary up with the sauce bottles? Rosemary I'm gonna have you move on now.

LEONARD: Sure.

ROSEMARY: Oh, okay.

LEONARD: You grab those ones. We fill them over here.

LEONARD *and* ROSEMARY *gather all the containers together, and begin refilling them.*

Ocean waves.

Everything is fine. I have a beach house—

ROSEMARY: Is this one for—

LEONARD: Tomato sauce.

Everything is—

ROSEMARY: Is this the sweet chilli?

LEONARD: Yup.

Everything is fine. I'm walking on the beach after a swim and I'm trying not to think about how much I hate my face … or my body … I just feel them. Yeah. I feel them in the balmy morning air. I'm wearing a clean white linen shirt that never gets sweaty or stained. I've like managed my underarm sweat situation. It's not, it's not a problem anymore.

LEONARD: **And I'm heading back to the house, where Mel has made coffee.**

We have an espresso machine, it was expensive but worth it, it's not going to break.

I sit in the breakfast nook—we have a breakfast nook—and I'm sitting in it with my coffee and I read the newspaper, a real newspaper, not on my phone, and I don't look at the bad news—there's no bad news, it's all good news, and I read it quietly and learn about the world, which is doing great, while Mel cooks breakfast.

Maybe we're low carb?

So yeah, she cooks eggs and avocado I feel great about it.

LEONARD *looks up.*

LEONARD: Everything fine?
ROSEMARY: Yup. Thanks.

ROSEMARY *is halfway through the first container when she realises she has put the put sweet chilli sauce into a tomato sauce bottle.*

ROSEMARY: Shit.

She dumps the sweet chilli from the bottle back into the larger container.

She realises that was a terrible idea and now there is bits of tomato sauce in the big container of sweet chilli.

Oh no.

Her breath quickens.

She gets a little sweaty.

She walks to the breakroom door and opens it.

She closes it and walks back.

She picks up the bottle and throws it in the trash.

She fishes it out of the trash.

She looks around.

Um.

ROSEMARY *pushes all the sweet chilli stuff to the side and starts refilling ketchup bottles.*

*She reaches for a bottle and instead pulls out **a My Little Pony figurine.***

She glances around. Everyone is working, they haven't noticed. **She gives the pony a kiss on the head. She feels a little better.**

TROY *enters with a clipboard which he reads from.*

TROY: Okay, so we're three minutes til doors so can we have a quick back of house meeting?

Great. Thanks.

So just a rundown of where we're all at.

- Welcome Rosemary, our newest team member.
- Ummm … trivia night is next Wednesday at the Bell Street store.

ROSEMARY: There's trivia night?

TROY: It's optional, but a pretty fun time.

LEONARD: It's just trivia about work. Like … they ask you questions about the employee manual and like Alto Bravo history.

ROSEMARY: What's Alto Bravo?

TROY: Did you do the online training modules?

ROSEMARY: Yeah.

TROY: It's a question.

RIVER: Alto Bravo owns us.

TROY: It's our parent company. They also own Hail Kale and Taco Standito. So your employee discount works at both of those too. This was all in the online training module.

ROSEMARY: Right.

RIVER: Anyway, you should come to trivia night Rosemary. There are prizes.

G.: Don't be fooled, the prizes are chocolate frogs.

ROSEMARY: I like frogs.

TROY: Can we focus?

Ummmmm …

As you know we are incredibly lucky to be one of the first stores in the nation to test the Five-S Kiosks.

The staff are unimpressed.

Okay sorry, I have to read that. I know everyone is frustrated with the kiosks, but let's just try to stay positive—

LEONARD: That's easy for—

TROY: Now is not the time, Leonard. Okay. Where were we, ummm …

G. *sighs and looks around. She would rather be anywhere but here. She silently wills* TROY *to shut up. It doesn't work.* **She looks out and finds her audience friend:**

G.: **He loves giving these speeches, you can tell.**

Reece always wins. He's a tool.

She watches TROY.

Look at him. He thinks he's inspiring us.

Lies.

**Stop. TROY STOP.
Stttooopppppp iiiiiiittttt.**

Ssssshhhhhhh.

TROY *continues briefing the staff.*

TROY: • Thank you for being part of this gigantic step towards a self-empowering customer service experience.

• The winners of last month's Gold Class Competition in this store were Reece and Amanda. So their photos will be on the board out front and they both get a Nespresso machine. The competition restarted yesterday so you've all still got a shot at the Nespresso machines for this month. I think the prizes will probably change next month, so …yeah … ummmm …

• If you'd like to donate to Brenda Waverly's support fund I'm currently taking collections.

Um, it says: 'Brenda is a beloved Assistant Manager at our Bell Street store and her partner was just diagnosed with stage 4 stomach cancer. Let's all help Brenda through this difficult time. Alto Bravo has agreed to match all donations made to the fund. So if you give one dollar, it's like you are giving two dollars. Your burger family is real family. We love you Brenda.'

• Also we have the Zesty Westy Ranch Burger happening for all of this month so make sure you're briefed on that, if you haven't made it before.

ROSEMARY: I haven't been briefed on the Zesty Westy.

TROY: It's fine. No-one orders it. Alright, we've got a school group at one, it's going to be a hectic day. River, is that a hand up?

RIVER: Yes. Did the school group pre-order?

TROY: Good question: No, due to an error with the MyBurger app they weren't able to

---

[*Back to her audience friend*]
Fuuuuuuuuuuuuucccckk.

I'm gonna tell you a secret: I'm not hungover. I didn't drink at all last night. I just played SIMS for too long, which basically has the same effect as drinking. Last night. Last night I played SIMS 2 for seven hours straight. I'm lying to you. It was nine hours straight. You don't judge me, right? I literally wish I was playing right now.

pre-order. Also two of the kiosks are down, and, look, we really should have another team member staffed, but we're gonna make it work!

Okay, so this morning make sure we're properly prepped! And we'll get through this together. Dream team! Love your work!

Oh sorry, there's one more thing

Shit, it never ends.

- They are looking for a new member of the Enthusiasm Committee, so if you're interested in that get in touch with Daron.

TROY: Um. Okay. River you're on fries, G. can I get you on dressing, and Leonard grill please.

LEONARD: I want to do dressing.

TROY: I need you on grill. And Rosemary you're gonna do buns. Have you done buns?

Ocean waves*. LEONARD *looks out.

ROSEMARY: I shadowed but I haven't done them on my own yet.

TROY: Leonard, could you walk Rosemary through it real quick? I'm gonna open the doors.

TROY *clicks on the sound system for the store. Canned music plays softly.* TROY *takes a set of keys from his pocket and exits to open the front doors. From this point forward food orders occasionally pop up on a screen and the Team Members fulfil them. In the down time they prep/clean/wait.*

LEONARD: [*to* ROSEMARY] So you look at the patty to see what kind it is and then you grab the correct size bun from here. See they have been pre-sliced. So for chicken we steam them in the steamer and for beef we toast them in the toaster. And you have to make sure you get the right kind for the right patty. Sesame for beef, no sesame for chicken and then there's the different sizes.

ROSEMARY: How do you know what size?

LEONARD: Oh. It's colour-coded. So red is large sesame, blue is small sesame, green is no sesame. See.

ROSEMARY: Red, blue, green …

LEONARD: It's overwhelming at first, but you'll catch on eventually and then you won't be able to forget it. Like ever. I dream about it.

G.: Me too.

RIVER: Me too.

They work.

Ocean waves.

LEONARD: **Everything is fine. Peaceful. It's the perfect temperature. I have a beach house. And I'm sitting in my breakfast nook eating poached eggs and avocado while reading the paper. And the world isn't burning or dissolving. And it's really quiet, almost, it's almost too quiet, but that doesn't make me lonely anymore. I don't feel like my brain is shredding into pieces. I don't feel lost or sad.**

It's what life's meant to be.

It's simple.

No. It's comfortable.

And then I finish breakfast and put my dish in the dishwasher—we have a dishwasher and a system that we agreed upon that means dirty dishes don't pile up in the sink—and then I take a shower in the ensuite—

TROY *enters and tacks a piece of paper to the wall.*

TROY: New roster.

He exits. G. *checks the newly posted roster.* ***Perhaps she gives her friend a frustrated glance.***

LEONARD: **—and it's very clean, there's no hair in the drain, and we have very nice soap, and then yeah, after the shower I take a notebook out to the beach. I take my notebook out to the beach, where I sit calmly and I write down all my thoughts. And they aren't fucked up or angry or bleak thoughts. They are gentle**

and true and they tumble out of me. It's really exciting! I think, I think I might be on to something, oh wow, actually, actually it's kind of ground-breaking? It's, yes, it's about the moment when—

ROSEMARY *has put her first patty onto a bun.*

ROSEMARY: Okay Leonard. I put it on the bun. So do I …

LEONARD: Um. Okay. Great. So once the patty is on the bun you pass it over here to dressings.

ROSEMARY: Then what.

LEONARD: That's it. G. will dress it while you do the next bun.

ROSEMARY: Great.

LEONARD: During rush we have three people here, one on buns and two on dressing, but when it's slow it's only one.

ROSEMARY: Right, cause dressing takes the longest.

LEONARD: Yeah. Dressing is the funnest job but it's second hardest after grill. And it can back up the whole line if you are slow on it, and then the burgers waiting to get dressed get cold and need to be remade. It's like the most important position. This one guy, Cyrus, I never worked with him, he moved to Perth, but apparently, he could handle buns and dressing all by himself on a Friday night.

ROSEMARY: Wow.

LEONARD: That's his picture right here.

ROSEMARY: Cyrus.

LEONARD *doesn't know if he's being ironic or not:*

LEONARD: Inspirational, right?

ROSEMARY: Yeah.

G.: [*interrupting*] Hey Leooonaaaard …

LEONARD: Yes, G.?

G.: Sorry. But. Can you cover for me next Wednesday evening? Pleeaaasse?

LEONARD: I have to study for exams.

G.: Right.

LEONARD: Sorry.

G.: Hey. River …

RIVER: I have my audition next Thursday so I need to focus the night before.

ROSEMARY: Oooo! What are you auditioning for?

RIVER: Music conservatories. I'm applying to three, and this is the first one.

ROSEMARY: Is this for uni?

RIVER: Yeah.

ROSEMARY: Singing?

RIVER: Piano.

ROSEMARY: I took lessons when I was little but I stopped and forgot everything. Don't stop.

RIVER: I won't.

ROSEMARY: You must be good.

RIVER: Yeah.

ROSEMARY: I can still play 'Für Elise'.

LEONARD: I can play 'Für Elise' too!

ROSEMARY: I love that song. Can you play that one River?

RIVER: I mean … Yes.

> *Pause.*

ROSEMARY: … Well I can cover for you, G. The kids are with my husband next week. Ex-husband. Sorry.

G.: Oh. Thanks. Maybe. I'll. Um. Have to check with Troy.

ROSEMARY: … Oh. Sure. That's fine … Just let me know.

> *Silence.*

LEONARD: How many kids do you have?

ROSEMARY: Just two.

LEONARD: Cute.

ROSEMARY: They are both being pretty high maintenance at the moment, so not that cute. But that's just. You know. Normal separation stuff, I think.

LEONARD: Separation from like—

ROSEMARY: From my husband. Their father.

LEONARD: Right.

ROSEMARY: I mean, at my age, why else would I be starting a new career where I have a twenty-year-old for a boss.

Sorry.

Nothing wrong with being twenty.

LEONARD: I thought maybe you just really loved burgers …

ROSEMARY: Ha. More like five months of separation after twenty-one years of—

LEONARD: TROY *enters.*

TROY: Damn it's hot today, isn't it?
LEONARD: Not really.
TROY: I think it's really hot.
LEONARD: Okay.
TROY: I think we need to open up some windows.
LEONARD: Do we have time for this?
ROSEMARY: What?
G.: Nothing. **Watch this, you'll love it.**
TROY: Rosemary can you take my keys, it's this one with the red thing on it, and go open up the windows out front. Just get some air happening in the place.
ROSEMARY: Of course.

ROSEMARY *exits.* TROY *cackles.*

LEONARD: It's really not that funny.
RIVER: I think it's funny.
LEONARD: It's really not.
TROY: Leonard could you give the floor a dry mop real quick?

LEONARD *mops.*

Does it smell like really like beefy in here today?
G.: It's a burger restaurant.
TROY: I mean like extra beefy. Like rotting beef. It's making me nauseous.
G.: It smells like the normal beef smell that it always smells in here.

ROSEMARY *re-enters.*

ROSEMARY: I can't find the keyholes.
TROY: The what?
ROSEMARY: The keyholes.
TROY: The what?
ROSEMARY: The keyholes. Like the holes for the keys. On the windows. The keyholes?
TROY: Oh. It's on the bottom. The bottom left I think.
ROSEMARY: Okay. I'll. Go check again.
TROY: Great thanks.

ROSEMARY *exits.* TROY *cracks up. So do* G. *and* RIVER.

LEONARD: Ugh.

TROY: Keyholes? Keyholes.

They wait.

ROSEMARY *enters.*

ROSEMARY: Yeah, no I can't find it.

TROY: Find what?

ROSEMARY: The keyhole.

TROY, G., *and* RIVER *can't contain their laughter.*

ROSEMARY: Why are you all laughing?

LEONARD: They are being assholes.

TROY: There's no keyhole.

ROSEMARY: What?

LEONARD: The windows don't open.

ROSEMARY: Oh.

LEONARD: It's a prank that's not very good that he plays on everyone.

ROSEMARY: So they don't open at all?

TROY: [*laughing*] No.

ROSEMARY: Oh.

She digests this information.

That's funny!

She genuinely appreciates a good prank.

Oh my god. Were you dying when I was like 'where are the keyholes?!'

TROY: Yes oh my god you kept saying it. Like 'the keyholes, the holes, the holes for the keys, the keyholes!'

ROSEMARY: That's a good one. That's a really good one!

TROY *hold his hand out for a fist bump.*

TROY: It's hard being new. Love your work, though.

They work.

There's definitely meat rotting somewhere. Did they take out the bins last night?

LEONARD: I don't smell anything.

RIVER: I think this happens to vegetarians. Like they feel sick from meat smells.

G.: Who's a vegetarian?

RIVER: Troy.

LEONARD: Since when?

TROY: What? Like. Always. I mean, like six years? Seven years.

G.: [*to audience friend*] **This is too much.**

And you knew this River?

RIVER: No! I mean, I. We had to share three personal facts at the Upper Leadership and Management Training Session.

LEONARD: Why are you a vegetarian Troy?

TROY: Lots of a reasons. It's better for you. It's better for the world. For animals. I have a video about it I can send you.

G.: No. I refuse to watch your video.

ROSEMARY: I'll watch it.

G.: Don't. It's a factory farm video that all the vegetarians try to make you watch.

TROY: It will change the way you see the world.

G.: I don't want to change.

TROY: The world would be a better place if we all ate less meat.

LEONARD: You're the manager of a burger restaurant.

TROY: Um, I know.

LEONARD: Your pay cheque—like everything you own comes from meat.

TROY: Are you a vegetarian?

LEONARD: Fuck no.

TROY: Yeah, see?

LEONARD: See what?

TROY: At least I try, you don't even—

Look, I don't have time for this. That order's been up for like ninety seconds. Is someone gonna make it?

LEONARD: Fine.

They work.

A moment.

TROY: **So on the news it's saying there's gonna be a flood. Yeah. The radio is all**

RADIO: **There's gonna be a flood.**

TROY: **Yeah. It's like. It's saying**

RADIO: **Get ready, like stock up on food and stuff. Or get out, evacuate.**

TROY: **And I don't wait to be told a second time. I go to the store and get**

> **Bottled water**
> **Dehydrated food and stuff**
> **Flashlights**
> **Batteries**
> **An inflatable raft**
> **A bow and arrow**
> **Tranquilizer darts**
> **Those tinfoil blanket things**
> **A camping stove**
> **Baby wipes**
> **And I go home, I go home, I go home and I sit in my bedroom with my dog (I have a dog) and I wait it out. And the storm is raging outside. There's rain and wind and thunder and water is rising all around my house. And then**
> **it passes.**
> **I made it.**
> **I made it through.**
> **I doze off. With the dog.**

He rests.

> **But then I wake up. Cause I hear someone calling for help. Oh god. They are like**

SOMEONE: **Help! I need help!**

TROY: **Shit.**

He wants to help but he's scared.

The whole situation is terrifying.

SOMEONE: **HELP!**

TROY: **Just hang on!**

LEONARD: Look Troy.

> LEONARD *holds up a beef patty.*

This used to be a cow and now it's your rent money.

TROY: Can you get back to work please?
SOMEONE: **HELP! Please help.**
TROY: **I'm coming! I'm coming to help you!**

> **TROY** *picks up an axe and heads to the door. He's a hero.*

LEONARD: Sure you don't want a bite?

> *The screams intensify.*

TROY: **Fuck you Leonard, I'm trying to help!**
Sir? Hello?! Where are you? I can't find you! I want to help, but I don't know where you are!

> TROY *is staring at the wall. Not moving.* ROSEMARY *notices.*

ROSEMARY: Troy?

> *He's startled.*

Sorry. I was just. Making sure you're okay.
TROY: I'm so fine.
ROSEMARY: Okay.

> *Pause.*

So what do you do, Troy?
TROY: What do you mean?
ROSEMARY: Like are you in school or something?
TROY: No.
ROSEMARY: Right.
TROY: Should I be?
ROSEMARY: Oh no, I was just wondering.
TROY: Right.
ROSEMARY: So you like it here?
TROY: Been here almost seven years.
ROSEMARY: Wow, that says a lot.
TROY: Yeah. People talk crap, but it's a good job.
ROSEMARY: That's great.
TROY: Good company, good people.
ROSEMARY: Really?
TROY: I mean yeah. I've never had any problems.
ROSEMARY: Right.
TROY: Yeah. And after two years you get stock options.

ROSEMARY: Good to know.

And where are you from?

TROY: What do you mean?

ROSEMARY: Like, are you from here originally?

TROY: I don't like answering that question.

ROSEMARY: Oh. Okay …

Pause.

TROY: I just get asked it a lot.

ROSEMARY: Fair enough. [*Pause*] What about you Leonard?

LEONARD: What?

ROSEMARY: Where are you from?

LEONARD: So I was born in Albury but we moved to Melbourne when I was five. Oh, but then we moved BACK to Albury for a year when I was eight. No. Sorry we moved to Melbourne when I was six and then back to Albury when I was eight and then back to Melbourne a year later and—

TROY: There's two orders up. Thank you, Leonard.

Pause.

ROSEMARY: I'm from here. Always lived here.

RIVER: Me too.

ROSEMARY: Oh wow.

G.: **Good talk.**

They work.

A moment.

Suddenly, the power goes out. The radio turns off. Silence. Then, someone is screaming for help.

SOMEONE: **Help! Please! Someone help!**

TROY: **It's an old man. He's trapped under a tree.**

Sir? Sir, it's okay. I'm going to help you, I promise.

I just … ummm … I'll just … I'll move this tree.

Okay.

TROY *pushes against the tree. It doesn't budge.*

It's really heavy. Sorry.

He tries some more. The screaming continues.

It's not working.

Okay. Okay. What do we—what do we do?

Can you, sorry, can you stop like crying? Just for a second. I'm sorry. It's like—I can't, I'm sorry, I just I really can't like, think, god, I—

The screams stop.

Oh shit. Sssshiiiiit.

Okay. Okay. Shit. Shit.

I had CPR training. Okay.

TROY *tries to revive the man.*

It's not working.

He's limp.

His eyes are open. And.

He's dead.

And I realise it's not. It's not an old man. It's actually. It's actually my brother. And I didn't save anyone and he's dead.

I didn't. I didn't save him so I run the fuck away, through the flood waters because I'm a shitty scared person that can't help anyone. And I don't have dog. I'm just alone and scared and helpless.

LEONARD: **Everything's fine.**

TROY *takes some deep breaths.*

TROY: **Stop it. Don't be negative. You have a choice.**

LEONARD: **I'm on a beach.**

TROY: **It's starting to rain again.**

LEONARD: **It's cloudy.**

TROY: **And I choose action.**

LEONARD: **It's the perfect temperature.**

TROY: **I choose to have a dog.**

LEONARD: **I'm writing in my notebook, I'm on a roll.**

TROY: **I find a boat, and me and the dog climb into it.**

The wind is picking up

LEONARD: **There's a breeze**

TROY: **and the water is rising.**

LEONARD: **and the water is rising**

TROY: **It's awful.**

LEONARD: **It's beautiful. The water swells towards my feet and I'm inspired.**

TROY: **I'm paddling as fast as I can.**

LEONARD: **It's rising faster and faster.**

TROY: **And I see someone in the distance.**

LEONARD: **It's a little scary, actually.**

The wind rushes. TROY *shouts to be heard.*

TROY: **Anyone out there?**

LEONARD: **I'm just doing some thinking.**

TROY: **It's dangerous.**

LEONARD: **I didn't realise.**

TROY: **Get in the boat. I'll take you to safety.**

LEONARD: **No. No. I don't … I don't think I need, um …**

TROY: **I killed my brother.**

LEONARD: **What?**

TROY: **He's dead. My brother is dead.**

LEONARD: **I'm sure you didn't, you didn't kill him, did you?**

TROY: **I couldn't. I couldn't save him. But I can save you.**

LEONARD: **No. Um. I have a beach house, it's just over—**

TROY: **Home isn't safe.**

LEONARD: **What? Yes it is. My home is safe.**

TROY: **No. Wrong. Sorry. You need to get in the boat.**

LEONARD: **Um. Okay.**

LEONARD *reluctantly gets in the boat.*

G.: Did we get more barbeque sauce?

TROY: It came in the morning delivery.

G.: It's not here.

TROY: What?! They did the same thing last week. This is so annoying. I'll call them.

TROY *exits,* *abandoning* LEONARD *in the boat.*

LEONARD: **Where are you going?**

No answer.

Is … is it safe now?
Can you drop me off at my house?

Everything is fine.

Everything is fine.

It's the perfect temperature.

My beach house is … it's big and calm and safe. It makes sense there. The whole world makes sense. We watch TV at night on one of those TVs that's a mirror when you turn it off. But we don't watch *The Block* **anymore. We watch like … classy TV …**

LEONARD *watches in awe as the world around him floods.*

But it floods.

The whole house.

Filled with water. The television is ruined. And it was very expensive.

Sunk. All of it.

Literally to the bottom of the ocean.

And I don't have insurance.

TROY *enters.*

TROY: Okay, this was supposed to have no pickles.

G.: Oh sorry.

TROY: Not your fault. Kiosk error.

G.: I'll remake it.

TROY: Bin this one please.

ROSEMARY: Wait, no I'll keep it.

TROY: What? No sorry.

ROSEMARY: What?

TROY: You can't keep it. You can use your staff discount to buy one on your break though. Thirty percent off. Then it will be fresh.

ROSEMARY: I don't mind not fresh.

TROY: It's just policy. You get thirty percent off. Not free food.

ROSEMARY: Even if you're throwing / it away?

TROY: Even if I'm throwing it away.

ROSEMARY: Okay. Got it. Sorry.

RIVER: Give it to me. I'll take care of it.

RIVER *throws it in the bin.*

TROY: Leonard. Why is the floor sticky? Wet mop please. I don't have time to be your mum today.

TROY *exits.*

LEONARD *sits in the boat, upset.*

A moment.

RIVER: We put a box in the bin.

ROSEMARY: What?

RIVER: Don't say anything to Troy, but we put a box in the bin and we put the reject burgers in the box and then we take them out back and eat them.

G.: It's the only rule River will break.

RIVER: I don't like wasting food.

G.: She doesn't mind any of the other bullshit though.

RIVER: I just agree with the other rules.

LEONARD: You agree that I should be written up for wearing coloured socks.

RIVER: They had skulls on them.

LEONARD: So?

RIVER: It's offensive.

LEONARD: To who?

RIVER: Customers.

LEONARD: We're back of house.

RIVER: I'm not arguing about this.

G.: It seems like you are.

RIVER: No, I …

LEONARD: I'm taking out the bin.

RIVER: Just one moment Leonard. Someone else might want it. G.? Would you like the burger?

G.: I'm good.

RIVER: Rosemary?

ROSEMARY: No thank you, hon—sorry. No thank you.

RIVER: And I'm also not hungry. Okay, Leonard. It's all yours.

LEONARD: Great thanks.

LEONARD *exits.*

G.: [*to* RIVER] Intense.

RIVER: What?

Music plays, but it's a little fucked up this time.

RIVER *gulps down the bottle of MPC.*

A little moan.

RIVER: You're right. I am intense. And I'm going to get new clothes so everyone knows exactly how intense. I am going to get different clothes, better clothes, that make me look hot, and maybe my nails done, long nails, and when people see me, they'll be like, she looks intense. Maybe also lip injections and a tattoo once I'm eighteen, a tattoo here. Of a horse. Like a vampire horse. And you will notice it peeking out from under my clothes when I dance at, like, at the clubs.

Maybe RIVER *suddenly has a tattoo of a horse? She dances, she's at the club.* G. *approaches* RIVER.

G.: You're so intense.

G. *grabs* RIVER *around the waist, and kisses her passionately. It's like a movie or a photograph.*

RIVER: Yes. Yes. This happens. You kiss me.

G.: I like your tattoo. Vampire horse; That's cool.

RIVER: Yes. You definitely say that. And. And then. And then we're doing it. Sex. We are having sex. Yeah. And it's not like internet porn. It's better. It's better than internet porn. And I've got black underwear on that I bought with Dad's credit card which I stole, because who cares! And then yeah we're touching parts. We're putting parts in parts. And kissing. Always kissing. And you're like:

G.: You're really pretty.

RIVER: No. No. Not that. You say 'You're so hot,' you say that to me.

G.: You're so hot, River.

RIVER: Yeah. And then I'm like 'Don't call me River.' And you're like 'What should I call you?'

G.: What should I call you?

RIVER: Wormslut.

G.: Wormslut?

RIVER: I saw it online.

G.: That's super hot.

RIVER: Yeah. It's so hot. So we're kissing kissing kissing kissing and the parts in the parts and you are calling my name, but my name is Wormslut and then … we both orgasm. At the same time. It's hot. It's so hot. Don't you think?

G.: **Ummm …**

RIVER: **You think it's hot!**

G.: **Yes. So hot!**

RIVER: **And then we sleep. We sleep all tangled up. And then we wake up. And. And we have brunch. And it's bagels.**

> TROY *enters.*

TROY: They'll send the barbeque sauce tomorrow, so today just get by with what we have left okay, **Wormslut?**

> **RIVER** *is euphoric.*

RIVER: **Yes. Okay. Everyone hear that? We're gonna skimp on barbeque sauce today. Rosemary, could I get you to fucking chop the shit out of some little red tomatoes?**

ROSEMARY: Yup.

> *She walks to the wrong piece of machinery.*

RIVER: Over here.

ROSEMARY: Yup.

TROY: Where's Leonard?

RIVER: Taking out the bins.

TROY: For how long? That chicken burger has been on the screen for like four minutes.

RIVER: Okay. I'll just—

TROY: I'll do it.

> TROY *makes the burger like a boss.*
>
> ROSEMARY *chops tomatoes.*
>
> LEONARD *returns, sated.*

Chicken burger's done.

LEONARD: Oh. Thanks. I was just—

> TROY *notices something out of the corner of his eye.*

TROY: Hang on, sorry.

> *He walks up behind* ROSEMARY.

Has someone shown you how to chop tomatoes before?

ROSEMARY: What?

TROY: Did you go through orientation?

ROSEMARY: Yeah … I, um, I was—

TROY: Okay well this is set to six.

ROSEMARY: Right. Is that wrong?

TROY: Four-T, six-G, two-fresh.

ROSEMARY: What's that?

TROY: It needs to be set to four for tomatoes. These are way too thick.
Four for tomatoes, six for grilled onions, and two for fresh onions.
four-T, six-G, two-fresh.

ROSEMARY: Two-fresh. That's right. I—

TROY: No. Four-T.

ROSEMARY: What?

TROY: Four-T. Tomatoes. Four-T.

> *She's lost.*

ROSEMARY: Right.

TROY: We will need to bin these. And start over. Okay?

ROSEMARY: Yup.

TROY: G.?

G.: Yes?

TROY: Would you mind pausing whatever you're doing and chopping
tomatoes?

G.: Sure.

TROY: Is she doing okay on buns, Leonard?

LEONARD: Um. Yes. She's doing great.

TROY: [*to* ROSEMARY] I'll arrange for River to go over all this again
with you sometime today, but for now can you slice buns?

ROSEMARY: Slice buns. Yup.

TROY: Do you know how to do that?

ROSEMARY: Yup. No problem. How many should I slice?

TROY: Three crates to start.

ROSEMARY: Yup. Easy.

TROY: Thanks.

> TROY *exits.* ROSEMARY *wanders around the kitchen a bit, helplessly.*
> *She's trying not to cry. She looks under a couple of counters. She*
> *stands for maybe ten seconds panicking and then goes to* LEONARD.

ROSEMARY: Um. Leonard. Do you know where we keep the crates with buns?

LEONARD: Dry storeroom.

ROSEMARY: Is that over by the—

> ROSEMARY *points.*

LEONARD: Yup.

ROSEMARY: Thank you.

> ROSEMARY *exits.*

> *A moment.*

> ROSEMARY *returns with three crates of buns and tears in her eyes. She unpacks the crates and tries to get her feelings under control.*

PONY: **Are you okay?**

> ***This makes her start crying again.***

Shhhhh. Shhhhhh.

ROSEMARY: **I'm doing a bad job.**

PONY: **You are wonderful.**

ROSEMARY: **Thank you. But I'm not.**

PONY: **You fucking are. You're kind, and pretty, and creative—**

ROSEMARY: **No, no, I'm old and scared and dumb.**

PONY: **Hey, hey hey! Don't!**
Remember that little dance you used to do?

ROSEMARY: **What?**

PONY: **The the dance! The dance we used do when you were sad!**

ROSEMARY: **I think so.**

PONY: **How did it go?**

ROSEMARY: **I can't. It's a stupid dance.**

PONY: **No it's not, it's a beautiful dance! Come on Rosemary! Do it for me.**

> ROSEMARY *does the little dance.*

Yes! Yes! That's it!
Now sing the song!

ROSEMARY: **[*singing*] Don't be sad Rosemary**
Let your heart sing

> Don't be sad Rosemary
> You are a king
> Don't be sad, Rosemary
> One day you'll have everything

PONY: **You're amazing!**

ROSEMARY: **Thanks.**

> **I guess it just didn't pan out.**

PONY: **There's still time. You're only forty-four. You're not like fifty or something.**

ROSEMARY: **But everyone around me is so young. Look at their skin. Look how excited they are for the future. They have so much hope.**

PONY: **Little shits.**

ROSEMARY: **I know what every day is gonna be. Unless something bad happens. The only surprises now are terrible. I miss the nineties. I miss thinking the world was a pleasant place. I miss being told I could be anything I wanted.**

PONY: **Rosemary, look at me, look right here: You CAN be anything you want to be.**

ROSEMARY: **I just want to be … respected.**

PONY: **Boom. You are respected.**

ROSEMARY: **I'm toasting buns.**

PONY: **You can work your way up!**

ROSEMARY: **No-one gets ahead on a part-time, minimum wage job. That is not how it works.**

> **TROY** *enters.*

PONY: **Look at him. Look. You could be his boss. Tell him. Fucking tell him what to do. Tell him.**

> **ROSEMARY** *looks at* **TROY.**

ROSEMARY: **I can't.**

PONY: **Don't say can't. Don't fucking say can't. Yes you can. Yes you can, Rosemary.**

ROSEMARY: Hey. Um. Troy. Could you … could you take these empty crates out back?

> TROY *is blindsided. He doesn't know how to react so he just complies.*

TROY: Um ... Yeah. Okay.

It's weird.

ROSEMARY: Thanks Hon.

PONY: **What a dickhead.**

TROY *exits a little dumbstruck by the interaction.*

Pause.

ROSEMARY: Okay. That's all the buns sliced.

RIVER: Great.

There's no more orders.

ROSEMARY: So ... now I just ...

RIVER: Wait for orders.

ROSEMARY: But there's none.

LEONARD: There's always a lull around eleven.

ROSEMARY: What do we do?

LEONARD: Just stand here and wait.

They stand around aimlessly.

A moment.

ROSEMARY: I'm actually starving.

G.: River has biscuits.

RIVER: I threw them away. Sorry.

ROSEMARY: I'll be okay.

LEONARD: I thought you hated wasting food.

RIVER: They were gross.

G. *is silent.*

RIVER *slaps herself and breathes a sigh of relief.*

Pause.

More standing.

A moment.

G. *lights a (perhaps imaginary?) cigarette. She leaves the kitchen and sits next to her audience friend. She offers her audience friend a drag.*

A moment. A casual conversation in confidence:

G.: **I'm an asshole.**

I don't know why I'm an asshole, I keep telling myself to stop being an asshole, but I can't stop.

I can't tell if it's me, or literally everyone else in the world.

I guess it's probably me.

I don't know what to do.

Like.

In general.

I'm just hanging out here like waiting for something interesting to happen, but nothing interesting has ever ever happened. I'm not talking about burgers right now I'm talking about my life. Like my entire life. I finished high school and now what? Now I just work? Until I die? How long does this last? You know? What am I supposed to do with all this time?

I don't really … have any … like … passions. Unless you count Sims, which I don't.

You know about the Sims, right? It's a life simulation. It's the best video game of all time. You create people and then you help them live their lives.

Like, I've made a Sim for everyone here. Except her.

She points to ROSEMARY.

Yet. And so you have all these people you've made and then you guide them through life and they follow your instructions. You can be kind or you can be cruel.

Want to know something fucked up?

I do terrible things. To my Sims.

I made Leonard have like sixteen children. I also make him piss himself. Frequently. And I make River dance until she cries.

Sims music plays faintly. Maybe RIVER *dances like a Sim?*

Oh shit, when I get home tonight, I'm gonna make Troy eat like twelve burgers. Fucking vegan video bullshit.

TROY *picks up a burger and takes a bite.*

I also have a Sim for myself.

I torture her sometimes too.

'Cause I'm fair.

If you don't play, you should. It's really … soothing.

Sometimes I feel like my Sim is the real me and I am the Sim. Like I prefer my life in the computer. Whereas Sim G., I think, wants out. She looks at me through the screen and waves sometimes like … 'help'.

She waves.

She doesn't know how good she has it.

She puts out her (imaginary?) cigarette.

The Sims spell is broken. TROY *wakes up from his burger eating trance. He looks at the burger, confused. He carefully spits out what's in his mouth into a napkin and stands, in shock.*

A cow wanders on stage.

COW: **What are you doing?**

TROY: **Oh shit.**

Sorry.

COW: **For what?**

TROY: **For like. You know.**

COW: **No. I really don't.**

TROY: **Like. For, ummm, eating you, and working here. And like. You know. Playing into that whole … like … you know …**

Factory farming.

COW: **You've been here seven years, man.**

TROY: **I know, I know.**

COW: **Look.**

He shows TROY *an open wound.*

TROY: **Oh Jesus. I'm so sorry. I just. I like. Have to make a living.**

COW: **I have to make a living as well.**

TROY: **I don't. I don't eat the food here really except the chips.**

COW: **Even the chips are killing me. Murdering me.**

TROY: **Yeah. Yeah. I do know that. I know that. I honestly. I'm just. I don't quite. Know. What to do. To like. Save you.**

COW: **Work somewhere else.**

TROY: **Like where?**

COW: **A vegan café or something?**

TROY: **My friend Bryce works at vegan café and they pay so bad man. Like thirteen dollars under the table. I wouldn't. I wouldn't be able to pay for my shit.**

COW: **A clothing store.**

TROY: **But. Like. Sweat shops.**

COW: **Not my problem.**

TROY: **See that. That is bullshit. You're just. You're just like self-serving. Just like everyone.**

COW: **I am one of God's creatures and this place is fucking hell and you are a slave in it.**

TROY: **I AM ONE OF GOD'S CREATURES TOO.**

    FUCK.

    Sorry.

    I'm just so sick of this holier than thou bullshit.

    We make food that's affordable and I'm sorry, it's—I'm really sorry, but this is just true—it's fucking delicious. And anyone can come in to this place anywhere in the world and order food and it's going to be cheap and taste good and we aren't going to make them feel dumb or judged or like they should be eating something better or more expensive or healthier or whatever. They can come in drunk or hungover or with their kids or on their own or with a ziploc bag full of change or wearing an evening gown and we will make them the same burger as we make for anyone, the same burger we made for them when they were six years old we will make for them when they are sixty. It's easy, its everywhere, it's non-judgemental. AND THEN ADDED BONUS you get to blame the entire world's problems on us. On me.

COW: **You should work in marketing.**

TROY: **Thank you.**

COW: **You are a terrible person.**

    The cow explodes.

TROY: No! God, no!

    Everyone looks at TROY.

    Confusion. A baby cries in the distance.

LEONARD: **About fucking time.**

TROY: **What?**

LEONARD: **You left me here in this boat with your dog.**

TROY: **I don't have a dog.**

LEONARD: **You said it wasn't safe.**

TROY: **Oh. Right. Sorry.**

LEONARD: **What is that sound?**

TROY: **What?**

LEONARD: **It's coming from that building over there.**

TROY: **Which one?**

LEONARD: **The one that looks like it's about to collapse.**

TROY: **Wait here in the boat.**

LEONARD: **No, I want to go to the beach—**

TROY: **No, no the beach isn't safe.**

> TROY *bounds off.* LEONARD *waits in the boat.*

LEONARD: **Everything is terrible.**

It's a disaster. It's freezing. I don't have a beach house. I don't have a dishwasher or a TV that looks like a mirror when you turn it off and I don't write in a notebook on the beach. I live in a shack. Maybe not even that. I live in a gutter and bathe in the polluted rain so I'm always sticky and cold and my teeth hurt but I can't go to the dentist and people come outside their big warm buildings and tell me to move on because I scare away customers. And I'm hungry. I'm always hungry. Nothing, nothing makes sense, there are no thoughts, because I'm just hungry, and alone, I have nothing, not a single thing, and my stomach hurts, and I'm not low carb, because I eat anything, anything I can find, because I'm so hungry that my whole life, my whole life is about food now.

> TROY *returns with a baby wrapped in a foil blanket.*

TROY: **I saved it. It's a baby. We need to get to the evacuation centre. Here, hold it.**

> LEONARD *takes the foil blanket.*

LEONARD: **This isn't a baby. This is a just a bunch of meat in a foil blanket.**

TROY: **What?**

LEONARD hungrily eats some of the meat.

TROY: **No, please, no don't, don't eat that.**

LEONARD: **I'm sorry. I was hungry. I … I have to go, I'm sorry …**

LEONARD gets out of the boat and wades through the flood water.

G.: I think we're out of large sandwich wraps.

RIVER: There should be another box.

G.: It's empty.

G. looks for another box of sandwich wraps.

TROY: **[*to* G.] Did you lose something?**

G.: I think we're out of large sandwich wraps.

TROY: **Do you need rescuing?**

G.: Um. I mean, **I … Yes.**

TROY: **Get in the boat.**

G.: **Oh … Okay.**

TROY: **I've been out here all day, helping where I can.**

G.: **Wow.**

TROY: **Apparently the news wants to interview me.**

G.: **That's great, Troy.** I'm gonna check the storeroom …

TROY: **What??**

G. climbs out of the boat. She looks for sandwich wraps.

ROSEMARY *finds a microphone in a crate of buns. She is unsure of what to do with it.*

ROSEMARY: **Test test.**

TROY: **Are you here to interview me?**

ROSEMARY: **What? No. I just found this microphone.**

TROY: **And what do you have to say?**

She thinks.

ROSEMARY: **I don't know yet.**

PONY: **Sing them a song Rosemary! Sing to them like you used to sing to me.**

ROSEMARY: **What song?**

PONY: **Just sing from your heart. They will fucking love it.**

ROSEMARY: **Um. Okay …**

Music plays.

ROSEMARY: [*Singing*] **I am a jar**
without a lid
I don't know if this is
any good but anyway,
Long time ago, I was
just a kid
And I was taught,
And taught
And taught
And taught
And now I know all
the things,
all the things I should
know
But people keep
teaching me still
No matter how old I
grow
I'm so taught
I've been taught
You know what I'm
saying?
Baby,
I'm taught.
I've been looked at.
I've been told things.
I've been assessed and
I've been outlined
I've been bottled
And ignored
But mostly I've been
designed.
There is an eternity
inside me
That is incessant,
needy, it
goes on forever

RIVER *(as a SIM) dances.*
G. *stops looking for*
sandwich wraps and
watches this. G.*'s initial*
enjoyment slowly fades to
misery.

TROY *unsuccessfully tries*
to scale a wall with the
meat baby.

LEONARD *strips off his*
clothes as he searches for
the beach.

Occasionally someone is
briefly sucked back into a
work task.

So so much more
inside me
That your
headquarters can't
measure
I am flooding
I am undocumentable
I am new languages
Maybe you are too.
And we are running
Through dark tunnels
because
We all are
looking for the exit.
We can all decide at
any
moment
Whatever we want.
We can all change our
minds.
Like I am a poet now.
Yes, baby, we can
redesign
It all.
I think.
I'm not actually sure.

The following takes place during the song, it can be overlapped and arranged as needed:

G.: Oh shit this was supposed to be no onions.

LEONARD: Just pick them off.

G.: Yeah, fuck it.

LEONARD: **Sorry, is the … beach … this way?**

    G. *ignores him.*

  The beach?

    An interruption from singing:

ROSEMARY: **I don't know.**
LEONARD: **The beach.**

> RIVER *ignores him, continues dancing.*

G.: [*in desperation, to her friend*] **Will you just play me? Please? Just tell me what to do and I'll do it. Tell me when to work and eat and have children and sleep and fall in love and go to the toilet and shower and watch television and you can even kill me if you want. I'm an asshole, I admit it. I need help. I'm a loser asshole that no-one likes but I think with your help I could be better.**

> RIVER *looks up from her dance.*

RIVER: **Sorry. That's. I don't mean to interrupt. But. I feel like. I feel the exact same way.**
G.: **What?**
RIVER: **I'm a loser and no-one likes me. But like. When I'm around you, I feel like … better …**
G.: **River. I want you to listen to me okay?**
RIVER: **Okay, yes I'm listening.**
G.: **Good.**
> **I want you to hear this.**
> **You**
> **are pathetic.**
> **You're a child.**
> **Now go eat your fucking biscuits alone in your room.**

> *Maybe this last line echoes around the space.*

RIVER: **Yeah, okay, that … that makes sense …**

> G. *looks out at the audience.*

G.: **You're judging me.**
> **Whatever, don't care.**
> **You're not even real.**
> **I'm just … alone.**
> **We all are.**

> RIVER *bashes her head against the wall. It doesn't make her feel better. She tries again and again, but it's not working. She doesn't give up. She keeps trying until eventually she passes out.*

LEONARD: **Help! Does anyone know CPR?**

TROY: **I have CPR training!**

LEONARD: **She's hit her head. Please. There's lots of blood.**

> TROY *gets a bit woozy.*

TROY: **No. God. Sorry. I can't do this, sorry … I have a blood thing … I, um, I just need to lie down.**

> RIVER *wakes up and glares at* TROY.

RIVER: **You're useless.**

TROY: **Leave me alone.**

> ROSEMARY *finishes her song and looks to the others for applause.*

ROSEMARY: *[to* PONY] **They don't like it.**

PONY: **Sure they do.**

ROSEMARY: **Really?**
> **Did you? Did you like it?**
> **You can be honest.**

> *No-one knows what to say.*

RIVER: **Um. I mean. How do YOU feel about it?**

ROSEMARY: **I don't know. Kind of like. Nervous.**

LEONARD: **I think maybe I didn't fully understand it.**

RIVER: **What's it supposed to be about?**

ROSEMARY: **Ummm … It's about me and like … my life.**

LEONARD: **Wow. Yeah. There's a lot in there.**

ROSEMARY: **… Thanks.**

ROSEMARY: *[to* PONY] **You are a liar!**

PONY: **No! I'm your biggest fan.**

ROSEMARY: **You told me I was special! But I'm not special!**

PONY: **Don't you fucking say that. Don't talk like that. There is only one you, Rosemary.**

ROSEMARY: **No-one cares about me except me! I'm the only one who can see this amount of meaning and beauty in my own life. None of it! None if it matters to anyone else!**

PONY: **It matters to me! If you just keep believing in me. But you have to believe, Rosemary!**

ROSEMARY: **When I was little all I wanted was fifty of you! Fifty ponies so people would like me. I wanted some ease, man!**

I wanted the ease that comes with fifty ponies! But you are a piece of plastic. You're just a plastic lie. And I believed you for so long! I thought one day, it will all make sense. I felt it. Deep deep inside myself. It's all, it's all headed somewhere, you know. If I just. Keep going. If I keep going someone will notice and there will … there will be a reward. Like a reward I earned. But I'm too tired to keep trying. So. I give up! Fuck you! Fuck you My Little Pony!

ROSEMARY *destroys* PONY. *A struggle.*

PONY: **Never give up!**
ROSEMARY: **QUIET.**
PONY: **You can be anything you—**
ROSEMARY: **STOP. TALKING.**

It's over.

I quit.

She quits.

G.: **What's going on?**
ROSEMARY: **I just quit.**
LEONARD: **You can't quit.**
ROSEMARY: **Yeah. I can. I just did.**
LEONARD: **What are you gonna do for money though?**
ROSEMARY: **I'm not thinking about that.**
RIVER: **That's … a bad idea …**
ROSEMARY: **Do you want to join me? It's good here.**
TROY: **I'm paying off my car. I don't think I—**
ROSEMARY: **Fuck your car. Take the bus.**
RIVER: **My dad will be mad.**
LEONARD: **It just seems … completely unrealistic.**
ROSEMARY: **Oh, it is. I'm living in a fucking fantasy.**
LEONARD: **Wow. Ummm … Okay.**
ROSEMARY: **Okay?**
LEONARD: **Yeah. Yeah, I quit.**

He quits.

Oh wow. This IS amazing.
TROY: **Really? Okay. Okay. Then me too. I quit too.**

G.: **Same.**

> G. *sighs. Relief.*

RIVER: **Alright, fine, I quit.**

> *They all quit. It's so good.*
>
> *A moment.*

G.: **So … what now?**

> *Pause.*

LEONARD: **Wanna go to the beach?**
ALL: **Yeah/Definitely/Okay/etc.**

> *Ocean waves.*

RIVER: **Oh wow.**
LEONARD: **It's so peaceful.**

> *They walk out into the water.*
>
> *A moment.*

ROSEMARY: **The air is nice.**
G.: **It's the perfect temperature.**
LEONARD: **It really is.**

> *Pause.*

RIVER: **Waves are unreal.**

> *Pause.*

LEONARD: **So.**
RIVER: **So.**
ROSEMARY: **Should we make dinner?**
G.: **Yeah.**

> *From this point forward, the binary font rule no longer stands. No-one knows what the truth is.*
>
> *They make dinner.*
>
> *With their hands.*
>
> *They eat the dinner they made.*
>
> *It satisfies them.*
>
> *Later.*

G. *is washing dishes.*

RIVER *enters.*

RIVER: Look I picked all these strawberries. There were so many of them. I just picked as many as I could.

TROY: [*eating one*] Oh wow. I needed this right now.

ROSEMARY: It's so sweet.

G. *is still washing dishes.*

G.: Save some for me.

RIVER: We will.

G.: This is my least favourite thing.

ROSEMARY: What is?

G.: Washing up.

ROSEMARY: Really?

G.: Um yeah.

ROSEMARY: I like it.

G.: You like washing up?

ROSEMARY: Yeah.

I mean if you are in a hurry and it's just like one of the twenty things you have to do before you get the kids ready for bed then it's awful yeah, but if you have time, to you know … really savour it … and the moment is all yours. Then. It can be, you know. Serene. Just dipping these smooth things in and out of warm water and then lining them up neatly to dry.

Yeah.

I like it.

G.: Well … do you wanna do it?

ROSEMARY: I did them yesterday.

G.: So?

ROSEMARY: Well … okay.

ROSEMARY *does the dishes and enjoys it.*

They all gather around a fire while ROSEMARY *washes up.* RIVER *warms her hands:*

RIVER: That feels good.

TROY: Yeah, it's a little chilly tonight.

RIVER: Whose turn is it to start?

LEONARD: Mine.

RIVER: Leonard.

LEONARD: Okay. Um.

A long time ago. In like nineteen-hundred or something. In like. A cold wet village in Europe or America. There was a little boy. That's you Rosemary. Let's say you're the little boy.

ROSEMARY: Yes.

LEONARD: And he was an orphan or something. He had nothing.

ROSEMARY: Yeah I have nothing.

LEONARD: You have nothing and you cry silently every night under your single scratchy wool blanket as you look out the window at the moon or something.

ROSEMARY: Yeah I cry. Cause I'm lonely and I have nothing. I have no friends. No money. No hope.

RIVER: You're a little dirty. Like soot on your face. You work in like. A factory.

LEONARD: Obviously. You work in a factory. Even though you're so so young.

G.: A factory that makes like …

TROY: Mobile phones.

LEONARD: I mean that's … sure. You are getting like five cents an hour or something, and your foster parent people demand you give them seventy-five percent of that for room and board.

TROY: Yes!

G.: And you grow up thinking you're nothing. Just nothing. You grow up thinking you're … a machine. A machine for making mobile phones. A machine among hundreds, thousands of other machines. And you don't really. You don't know how to access anything other than the making part of yourself. The robot part of yourself.

TROY: But now you're an adult. In the world. You leave your evil foster parents and strike out on your own.

RIVER: And you work really hard. Because you don't know how to do anything else. Except work. You work really hard and you like. Make it. Somehow.

ROSEMARY: Or maybe I don't.

LEONARD: Yes. Maybe you don't. That's also a possibility. But let's say you do.

ROSEMARY: Okay fine.

LEONARD: You make it. And you start like. Your own factory. You make mugs. It's a mug factory.

RIVER: You have innovated. You have come up with amazing new ideas for mugs. You make like the best mugs.

LEONARD: Everyone wants your mugs.

RIVER: Yeah.

ROSEMARY: No yeah, I am at the top of the mug game.

TROY: Yes. You are. And you are in charge. You are in charge now of all these people. You, a little orphan.

RIVER: But your face isn't dirty anymore.

G.: No. You live in a big house with a swimming pool now. And you have kids that aren't orphans. You play with them on Sundays in the pool. You pretend to be mermaids.

LEONARD: Yeah. And you did all that with nothing but your skin and bones and determination.

TROY: Fucking amazing.

LEONARD: Yes. And then one day you are out in your yard and you hear something. A whimper in rosebushes.

G.: Or the jasmine.

LEONARD: The thick ivy covering the back wall of the garden.

G.: Yes.

TROY: It's like [*making a whimpering sound*]

LEONARD: Yes. And it scares you. The sound. It like stirs something deep inside you. Some little vulnerable child part of you. The most human part of you—because you are not quite human at this point in your life, you are a successful businessman machine who overcame, and also a good father with a beautiful garden and a great body, you work out. But this sound—it makes you feel small and real.

ROSEMARY: It makes me feel like I have soot on my face.

G.: And you hate that. You hate being small and real.

RIVER: You haven't felt that in years.

ROSEMARY: Yeah.

LEONARD: And so you screw up all your courage and you investigate. You walk over to the ivy and follow the sound and you reach your hands out and part the ivy and you find—

RIVER: A little baby bird—

TROY: That's what I was gonna say!

RIVER: Yes. A baby bird with no wings.

LEONARD: Yeah it's a baby bird with no wings. It was born that way. It can't fly.

G.: And you see this bird. And it. That child human part of you grows bigger. It's taking over your body. You're shaking and sweating and you're trying not to cry. You feel death all around you. You feel your heart beating and you realise how easy it would be for it to stop beating. Like it's keeping you alive but it could just stop, stop keeping you alive.

TROY: And you look at the bird's soft featherless skin and you look at your soft featherless skin and you think about how thin your skin is and how easy it would be to break it—how this soft thin skin is the only thing holding you together.

LEONARD: And you feel profoundly like a person—

G.: Yes! You remember that you aren't a robot and you look up at your mansion and you think about how it's not safe there, it's not safe anywhere. Like, the world is coming for you and your family and your kids and you remember the moon outside your childhood window, and that scratchy wool blanket, and your tears, and your dirty face, and they start pouring down your face these little tiny child-sized tears—

ROSEMARY: and I'm sobbing this high-pitched sob like [*demonstrating*]

LEONARD: and you hear yourself and that scares you even more—

RIVER: and you're like oh my god my kids are gonna hear me—

TROY: But you don't want that! You're like they can't hear me, they can't see me like this, I'm such a tiny miserable person, they will lose all respect for me, I have to hide, I have to like bury myself, I have to stop this right now.

LEONARD: And so you gently pick up that baby bird and you run outside of the walls of your mansion.

RIVER: Yes you run into the street—

TROY: and you live in like a really isolated rural area so there's no-one there, you're alone on the street—

G.: and you're holding this bird in your hand, it's small and warm and hairless and wingless, it feels like …

TROY: a ballsack—like it's like you're holding your own ballsack—

G.: Yeah. And you look down at the bird's fucked-up little body, you know that it cannot survive on its own.

RIVER: Yes.

ROSEMARY: And?

RIVER: And you throw it down onto the pavement as hard as you can.

ROSEMARY: Yes. And its little body is mangled and it's dead.

RIVER: And you feel better sort of and you go back home.

LEONARD: Yes. You go back home and you have cereal for breakfast.

They all sit for a moment, winded, unsure of what they created.

Pause.

TROY: I'm gonna go to bed.

ROSEMARY: Wait. We need more wood.

TROY: I'll do it in the morning.

ROSEMARY: The fire will go out.

TROY: I'm really tired. I think I'm getting sick.

ROSEMARY: Okay, fine. Leonard will you do it?

LEONARD: I did it last night.

ROSEMARY: Well we can't let it go out. It's cold tonight.

TROY: Why don't you do it Rosemary?

ROSEMARY: You know my back is fucked up. Leonard, please.

G.: Just listen to Rosemary, Leonard.

TROY: Why is she in charge?

G.: What do you mean?

TROY: We all listen to her like she's king or something.

ROSEMARY: Like I'm KING?

TROY: Yeah. Who elected her?

RIVER: Well kings don't get elected so—

TROY: I'm just saying I'm sick of you acting like you know everything Rosemary. Why are we all listening to you?

ROSEMARY: You don't have to listen to me. I'm just the one willing to be organised. I made a whole chore list so that we rotate fairly.

TROY: Yeah why are you making the list?

ROSEMARY: Cause no-one else was doing it.

TROY: What if I want to make the list?

ROSEMARY: Then make it.

TROY: No.

ROSEMARY: Well then—

TROY: But I also don't want it automatically to be assumed that it's you that gets to make the list.

ROSEMARY: Fair enough. If someone else wants to be in charge then I'm very happy—

TROY: So you admit it!

ROSEMARY: What?

TROY: You admit it! You just admitted it! Did you all hear that?

ROSEMARY: ADMITTED WHAT?

TROY: You said you were in charge. You think you're in charge.

ROSEMARY: Oh my god. I'm not in charge—

TROY: You think you're king!

ROSEMARY: If I'm in charge I don't want it. I don't want it. I just want everyone to help do the things that need to be done. I definitely don't want to be king. If you want to be king, then take it.

TROY: I just want to discuss it. I think that's a fair request.

ROSEMARY: Yeah, I guess it is.

>   *Pause.*

RIVER: So we're electing a king?

LEONARD: Can we stop saying king?

TROY: Queen?

G.: I'd much rather be king.

ROSEMARY: We're not electing a king.

LEONARD: Then what.

TROY: Someone who is more like … there to guide.

RIVER: Manager?

LEONARD: Gross.

G.: Just like. Um. A voice.

RIVER: Yes!

G.: A guiding voice.

LEONARD: Great.

RIVER: Okay we are electing a guiding voice.

G.: Great.

TROY: Great.

>   ROSEMARY *gives an accidental little sigh. They all look at her.*

RIVER: What is it?

ROSEMARY: Nothing!

RIVER: What?!

ROSEMARY: Just. This is a dumb idea.

G.: What?

TROY: So pessimistic.

ROSEMARY: You're right. Sorry. Keep going. Yes. Let's elect a guiding voice.

TROY: Ignore her.

ROSEMARY: Yes, please, ignore me.

RIVER: Okay. So who wants it.

LEONARD: I don't want it.

ROSEMARY: I don't want it either.

RIVER: G? What about you?

G.: Um. I don't know. Maybe.

RIVER: You know.

G.: I really don't know.

LEONARD: I think you should do it.

RIVER: Yes. Me too. If you want.

G.: I …

ROSEMARY: Yes. Actually. Me too.

LEONARD: Troy?

TROY: I mean. I'll do whatever the group wants.

LEONARD: G.?

G.: Yeah, fine. Okay. I'll. Be the guiding voice.

RIVER: Amazing.

LEONARD: So who should get the wood?

G.: Um. Right. Who doesn't mind getting the wood?

> *Pause.*

RIVER: I'll do it.

G.: Do you need help?

RIVER: No, all good.

G.: Easy. Yeah …

> RIVER *gets wood. They feed the fire.*
>
> *Time passes.*
>
> *The fire fades.*

The world grows colder.

They watch it happen.

The sun sets earlier now.

Everyone is uncomfortable.

RIVER: The fire's out.

TROY: Everything's damp. Nothing will burn.

> *Everyone wraps themselves in blankets, cardboard, whatever they can find.*

ROSEMARY: I'm actually starving.

LEONARD: Are there any more of those strawberries?

RIVER: No. Sorry.

> *The* COW *ambles in and stares at* TROY.

TROY: Oh my god.

LEONARD: Is that?

TROY: I know you.

G.: Oh my god.

TROY: What does it want?

G.: Troy.

TROY: What?

G.: You have to kill him.

TROY: What, why?

G.: Someone has to.

TROY: I. Look. I have a blood thing. Like if I see blood I …
    I just can't. I can't kill him.

G.: We're hungry.

> *Pause.*

TROY: Shit. Shhhhhiiiit.
    Okay. Um. Okay …
    Fuck.
    Don't. Like. Don't watch.

> *Everyone turns away.*

> TROY *readies himself.*

> *He kills the* COW.

It takes a while.

He's swearing and crying and apologizing the whole time. Something like:

Shit. Shhhhhit, sorry.
Oh my god sorry.
I feel a little … huuuhhhhhhghgghhh.
Okay. Okay. Here we go.
I'm sorry.
Shit.
Shit. Sorry, sorry.
Shhhhhit. Oh shit.

He emerges, covered in blood, with a plate of burgers.

Dinner.
ROSEMARY: Yum.

They eat.

G.: This is the best thing I've ever eaten.
ROSEMARY: Yeah.
RIVER: But the bun is wrong. It should be sesame and toasted.
LEONARD: I noticed that too.

They eat.

Should we play the stupid game?
ROSEMARY: Not again please.
G.: It's not fun.
LEONARD: That's why it's called the stupid game.
TROY: Okay. I'll go first. Um …
New shoes.
ROSEMARY: Fine.
Breath mints.
LEONARD: What?
ROSEMARY: You can't judge someone's turn.
G.: She's right.
LEONARD: Fine. Hot showers.
G.: Ummm … pillows.
LEONARD: Good one.
G.: Your turn River.

RIVER: What?

TROY: We're playing the stupid game.

RIVER: Oh. I don't know. This game is hard.

LEONARD: It's not.

G.: Just name something you miss. What about like. Milkshakes.

RIVER: I wasn't great with lactose.

Ummmm …

No I don't know.

I just. Am actually really happy here.

Yeah.

I don't miss being alone. And I don't miss being sad and scared for no reason.

LEONARD: Same.

TROY: What about not having sand everywhere. Do you miss that?

RIVER: A little. But not that much.

TROY: So uncomfortable.

RIVER: That's the thing though. I am so comfortable. I don't feel gross anymore.

ROSEMARY: You were never gross.

RIVER: I used to think about every word I said before and after I said it, and I don't do that anymore. And I used to think about sex just, like, all the time, and feel really really terrible about it. And now. I don't feel bad about it at all. And I used to have a huge crush on you [*gestures to* G.] and now I don't at all. Like thank god we were never together, you know?

G.: Oh.

Great.

RIVER: I know! You're just another person!

G.: That's true.

RIVER: I do miss the piano though.

ROSEMARY: Of course.

RIVER: And nail clippers. And Red Bull. I miss Red Bull so much.

G.: With vodka.

RIVER: Sure.

LEONARD: Whiskey.

ROSEMARY: I could go a beer right now.

G.: Let's do a cheers.

Everyone but TROY *raises an imaginary glass. They all look at him.*

TROY: I don't drink.

G.: Since when?

TROY: I've literally never had alcohol in my life.

LEONARD: God, why?

TROY: Cause um. My brother was like.

An addict.

RIVER: Oh wow.

TROY: Yeah. And he like. Died. From like. You know. It.

Awkward silence.

I found his body. And it was super like … disturbing? So, yeah, I don't drink.

LEONARD: I didn't know that.

TROY: Yeah, it's a weird thing to talk about so …

RIVER: We don't have to cheers.

G.: No.

Pause.

RIVER *shivers in the cold.* LEONARD *tries to revive the fire.*

G.: It won't work Leonard. The wood's too damp.

TROY: You know what I miss? Weirdly.

ROSEMARY: What?

TROY: Working.

ROSEMARY: Wow.

LEONARD: Hard disagree.

TROY: I know, I know, I know. But. I have like always, always worked. This is the first time in my life that I have had time to do … anything else.

I just miss knowing what to do. You know.

Pause.

G.: I get it.

TROY: Work was just. For me. A reason to get up.

LEONARD: Yeah, a FUCKED reason to get up. Remember catching the bus at six a.m.?

RIVER: And then making five hundred burgers.

LEONARD: But not even making five hundred burgers, just putting like exactly one thousand pickles on five hundred burgers.

RIVER: Just all day placing pickles.

G.: Remember the day there was the game at the oval AND the protest?

RIVER: Yes! That was so fucked!

TROY: We made one thousand and fifty-three sandwiches that shift.

ROSEMARY: That sounds terrible.

LEONARD: Oh it was terrible! It was so terrible!

G.: Like all these orders were coming in and in and in and we were all like thinking we were literally gonna die. But then there was this moment when we just … stopped panicking and we all clicked in and like got the impossible thing done.

RIVER: It felt like we won a war.

ROSEMARY: That's not actually a great feeling.

TROY: No. It was incredible. We were like one organism. One big burger-making organism. And if I moved my foot G. would move her hand. You know?

G.: Remember Leonard, how I would always be on dressing and you would get so mad about it?

LEONARD: They always put me on grill. It's reverse sexism. I hate grill.

RIVER: No. G. was just better at dressing than you.

LEONARD: What?!

RIVER: Yeah. Like with this team here, I'd put you on grill, G. on dressing, I'd be on fries so I could oversee everything and, Rosemaryyy—

ROSEMARY: I'm on buns, I know.

RIVER: Yes, exactly. Rosemary is on buns. And Troy would be coming in and out, telling Leonard to mop.

They begin to move around, role playing the memory.

G.: Yes, and we haven't prepped properly so we are behind and Troy is flipping out about it, but trying to play it cool.

TROY: Leonard, can you give the floor a quick dry mop?

LEONARD *is still trying to start the fire.*

LEONARD: I'm busy.

TROY: It's not gonna work, Leonard. Everything's too damp.

G.: Don't worry about him. I can mop.

She mimes.

RIVER: Figures of eight!

G.: Oh right, sorry.

She adjusts her mimed mopping to be in figures of eight.

RIVER: Okay, so after I filled the hopper I'd realise all the toppings bins need refilling so I'd have to chop tomatoes as fast as I could.

ROSEMARY: Four-T, two-G, six-fresh.

TROY: Oh my god. No.

ROSEMARY: What?

TROY: It's four-T, six-G, two-fresh.

ROSEMARY: Four-T, six-G, two-fresh.

TROY: Yes! Four-T, six-G, two-fresh.

ROSEMARY: Four-T, six-G, two-fresh, four-T, six-G, two-fresh, four-T, six-G, two-fresh …

Her attempt to burn the phrase into her memory turns into a chant. Everyone except LEONARD starts chanting along with her. They work and chant.

RIVER: Is that a Zesty Westy on the screen?

G.: I don't know how to make that.

RIVER: TROY!

TROY: What is it?

G.: We don't know how to make this Zesty Westy.

TROY: Do you have the ranch seasoning?

G.: No, where is the ranch seasoning?

TROY: This is why we brief you. I think there's some in the dry storeroom.

RIVER: Leonard can you check for me?

LEONARD: I'm not playing.

ROSEMARY: I can do it! Where is it?

TROY: With the sauces.

ROSEMARY: Right.

TROY: Love your work. It's the same as a regular roast chicken except you have the ranch powder, which I'll show you in just a moment, and also jalapenos which should be with the rest of your—

Then, a gasp.

RIVER: Um. I.

> RIVER*'s hand is covered in blood.*

> *The light changes: harsher, fluorescent. They are definitely not on a beach.*

Sorry. I. I cut myself. I'm sorry.

G.: Oh wow. Okay. Um. Troy.

TROY: What's up?

G.: So River cut herself.

TROY: There are bandaids in the first aid kit.

G.: Yeah. There's. There's quite a bit of blood. What did you cut?

RIVER: My fingers. My pinkie and my ring finger.

G.: Okay. Troy. What should we.

TROY: I. Oh. Wow. Is this really happening?

G.: Yeah, yeah it is, we need a towel.

RIVER: I got it, um, it's on the buns. I'm sorry. I'll pay for them.

> TROY *gets woozy.*

TROY: Okay … I'm feeling … Sorry, that's a lot of blood.

> *A pause. Blood drips down* RIVER*'s hands.*

G.: Sit down, Troy. Um. Okay.

> ROSEMARY *returns from the dry storeroom.*

ROSEMARY: I can't find the seasoning. Are you sure—

G.: Rosemary.

ROSEMARY: Oh god.

G.: Ummmm … who can. Like who knows about cuts. Leonard?!

LEONARD: What?

G.: We need your help.

LEONARD: I don't like this game.

G.: Leonard! You have to.

LEONARD: What?

> *He looks up.*

G.: Her fingers.

LEONARD: Shhhit. Okay. Hold it like this. Pressure. It will be okay.

RIVER: I should get more buns in case there's a rush.

ROSEMARY: I think don't worry about the buns just yet, hon.

RIVER: Should I see a doctor or something?

G.: Could someone call the hospital?

ROSEMARY: I can do it.

> ROSEMARY *exits.* TROY *breathes.*

> G. *bends down and picks something up from under a counter.*

G.: Leonard. I think that this is one of … um …

LEONARD: Okay. I'll get. Um. The cling wrap.

> ROSEMARY *enters on the phone.*

ROSEMARY: They are transferring me. I'm on hold. How old are you River?

RIVER: Seventeen.

ROSEMARY: We should call your parents.

> [*Into the phone*] Hello? Yeah my name's Rosemary and I'm …

> *She exits speaking on the phone.*

LEONARD: What's your locker combination? I'll get your phone and we can call your mum.

RIVER: My mum's dead.

LEONARD: Oh wow. I didn't know. Um. I. I'm sorry for your loss.

RIVER: No she died when I was like three. I don't even remember her. You don't have to be sorry.

LEONARD: Okay. I'll call. Um. Is your dad alive?

RIVER: Yeah.

G.: Tell him your locker combination.

RIVER: I. I can't remember. Three-six-nine-eight? Maybe?

> LEONARD *exits.*

I don't feel good.

G.: I know. You're gonna be okay.

> TROY *holds* RIVER*'s non-injured hand.*

TROY: Yeah you are.

> ROSEMARY *enters on the phone.*

ROSEMARY: They want to know how much blood.

G.: It's um. We have soaked through four Chux.

ROSEMARY: They have soaked through four Chux. Okay. Okay. Okay. Okay. / Thanks. Yes.

Of course. Yes. Okay. Okay. Yes. You too. I mean. Yeah thanks.

LEONARD: Okay got it. I'm calling the number labelled 'Daddy'. I hope …

RIVER: That's the one.

LEONARD: It's ringing. Hello? Oh it's voicemail. Should I leave a message?

G.: Yes.

LEONARD: Hi this is. Um. My name is Leonard, I work with your kid. She's hurt herself really really badly so just letting you know. Okay. Bye.

G.: Oh my god.

LEONARD: What?

G.: That's just. Nothing.

ROSEMARY: Alright they said they can send an ambulance, but it might be faster if one of us just takes her. It's only like five minutes away. I took the bus. So I can't.

TROY: I drove. I can take her.

G.: Really? … Did anyone else drive?

TROY: No. I can do it.

G.: Are you sure?

TROY: Yes. I feel. I feel like I can do this.

G.: Okay.

LEONARD: Here's the clingwrap with your um. Fingers. And your phone.

They all walk RIVER *out.*

TROY: You're gonna have to call corporate.

G.: Yeah we can do that.

TROY: Just tell them—

G.: We know what to tell them.

TROY: Love it.

The space is empty.

A moment.

Then G., ROSEMARY, *and* LEONARD *return. They are dirty and bloody and exhausted from everything that's happened. They stand, dazed for a moment.*

G.: Holy shit.

LEONARD: I know.

Pause.

ROSEMARY: Oh god.

What's she gonna do about her audition thing?

LEONARD: Oh shit, I didn't even think of that.

ROSEMARY: Medicine is so advanced. Right?

LEONARD: No. Not that advanced. It's not magic.

Pause.

G.: I gotta call corporate.

They clean. G. *calls.*

Of course.

Pause.

Yes.

Yes.

Pause.

Yes.

Pause.

Yes.

Pause.

Of course.

Yes.

Great.

Yes.

Yes.

Great. I'll—yes. Yes. Yes. I'll. I'll. I'll tell them. Yes. Yes. Alright yes.

She hangs up.

Ray says to temporarily close so they can come in and sanitize. I have to fill in the incident report, cash out, and put a sign on the door.

LEONARD: Oh. So …

G.: If everything is packed down, you can go home.
ROSEMARY: Okay.

    ROSEMARY *and* LEONARD *exit to the staffroom.*

    G. *stands alone for a moment holding the incident report form.*

    She looks out into the audience and catches the eye of her friend.

    LEONARD *and* ROSEMARY *come back with their bags etc.*

LEONARD: Do you work tomorrow?
G.: Yes.
ROSEMARY: Me too. Morning shift.
LEONARD: Same. I'll see you there Rosemary.
ROSEMARY: See you there.

    ROSEMARY *is checking her phone. She gives a little gasp.*

LEONARD: Are you okay?
ROSEMARY: No, yeah. Just … I won the Ooshie.
LEONARD: Wow. Congrats.
ROSEMARY: Connor is gonna be so happy.

    ROSEMARY *exits.* LEONARD *hovers.*

G.: Are you okay?
LEONARD: … I don't think so.
    I just … really don't like this place.
G.: Yeah.
LEONARD: Are you okay?
G.: I don't know.
    I fucked up.
LEONARD: We all did.
G.: Yeah.

    LEONARD *exits.*

    Ocean waves.

THE END

RED STITCH | THE ACTORS' THEATRE

presents

Fast Food

13 MAY–5 JUNE 2022

Playwright
Morgan Rose

Director and Production Dramaturg
Bridget Balodis

Set and Costume Design
Sophie Woodward

Lighting Design
Giovanna Yate Gonzalez

Sound Design and Composition
Danni Esposito

Lighting Design Mentor
Katie Sfetkidis

Dramaturgs
Tom Healey and Ella Caldwell

Stage Manager
Rain Okpamen

Assistant Set & Costume Designer and Assistant Stage Manager
Max Bowyer

Assistant Director
Kevin Hojerslev

Troy – **Kevin Hofbauer**

G – **Lucy Ansell**

River – **Chi Nguyen**

Leonard – **Casey Filips**

Rosemary – **Ella Caldwell**

This play was developed through Red Stitch's INK writing program.

RED STITCH | THE ACTORS' THEATRE

Artistic Director
Ella Caldwell

General Manager
Fiona Symonds

Production Manager
David Bowyer

Front-of-House Manager
Penelope Thomson

Development Manager
Patrick Fitzgerald

Marketing Partner
A Good Plan Group

RED STITCH ENSEMBLE

Ella Caldwell
Richard Cawthorne
Jung-Xuan Chan
Jessica Clarke
Kate Cole
Brett Cousins
Ngaire Dawn Fair
Daniel Frederikson
Emily Goddard
Kevin Hofbauer
Justin Hosking
Darcy Kent
Caroline Lee

George Lingard
Chanella Macri
Olga Makeeva
Dion Mills
Christina O'Neill
Joe Petruzzi
Dushan Philips
Tim Potter
Ben Prendergast
Kat Stewart
Sarah Sutherland
Andrea Swifte
David Whiteley

BOARD

Sophia Hall (Chair), Damon Healey (Treasurer), Henrietta Thomas (Secretary), Ella Caldwell, Catherine Cardinet, Humphrey Clegg, Andrew Domasevicius-Zilinskas, Belinda Locke, Michael Rich, and Sandra Willis.

We at Red Stitch acknowledge and pay our respects to Australia's First Peoples and Elders past and present, and offer our gratitude to the Boon Wurrung and Wurundjeri Woi Wurrung peoples of the Kulin Nation, on whose unceded lands we work.

THANK YOU

This development and production of *Fast Food* would not have been possible without the generous support of our donors and partners

KINDRED DONORS

Brian Goddard (in Memoriam)
The Lionel & Yvonne Spencer Trust
Maureen Wheeler AO & Tony Wheeler AO
Lyngala Foundation
Per & Ingrid Carlsen
Sieglind D'Arcy
Andrew Domasevicius & Aida Tuciute
Carrillo Gantner AC and Ziyin Gantner AC
John Haasz
The James Family Charitable Foundation
The Madeleine & Ed Neff Family Foundation
The Kate & Stephen Shelmerdine Family Foundation
Rosemary Walls
Anonymous
Beth Brown
Elise Callander
Caitlin English
Linda Herd
Graham & Judy Hubbard
Liz & Peter Jones
Michael Kingston
Alex Lewenberg
Jenny Schwarz
Christina Turner & Lyle Thomas
Jenny Veevers
Anita & Graham Anderson
Angela Benic and Peter Matkovic
Michael Brindley & Karinn Altman
Robin Carter

Julie & Ian Cattlin
Timothy Clark
Sophia Hall
Damon Healey
Edwina Mary Lampitt (in Memoriam)
The Lewis Langbroek Charitable Endowment
Barbara Long
Kate & Peter Marshall,
Kaylene O'Neil
Timothy Roman
Craig Smedley
James Syme,
Jane Thompson & Chris Coombs
Tony Ward & Gail Ryan
Ian & Grace Warner
Graham Webster & Teri Snowdon
Margaret Yuill

MAJOR PARTNERS
Creative Victoria
City of Port Phillip
Cybec Foundation
Portland House
Lyngala Foundation
Malcolm Robertson Foundation
Playking Foundation
Copyright Australia Creative Development Fund

Rear 2 Chapel Street, St Kilda East, VIC 3183
http://redstitch.net/ | FB: @RedStitchTheatre | T: @redstitch
boxoffice@redstitch.net | 03 9533 8083

WRITER'S NOTE

I don't know.

I don't know what to write here.

Ughhhhhnszfdnksalckvlweklyyyydfkl dkzcs;lddwuuuhhhh.

I started this piece thinking I was writing about the refuge of the human imagination in a shitstorm. I told everyone it was about how we can fantasize about anything we want, and no-one can stop us. It was meant to be joyful and uplifting. That was in 2018. Then we were all plagued by the plague. In the two years I spent locked in my apartment fantasizing about not being in my apartment while ordering Stuff at 11pm from fucking Amazon so that I could feel something, the play took a turn towards something darker. I couldn't stop it from happening, I guess I didn't really try.

To attempt to make up for the fact that I didn't deliver joy, I'll say this: People are great. My chest literally aches with how great they are. And even though we ruin a lot of things, even though we made up assembly lines, and money, and class, and factory farming, and red dye #40, and plastic toys children are meant to collect to feel good about life, we did it all because we were trying really hard to imagine something beautiful. It didn't work out in the case of the assembly line, but I still have hope. Because we can imagine in any direction we want.

This text was created with the direct input of a whole parade of smart kind folks. Thank you from the depths of my loins to: Kat, for everything, always. Ella and Tom, for your calm and skill and brilliance. Bridget, I trust and admire you so much, everybody does. Kevin Hofbauer and Chi Nguyen for creating and informing the characters with your brains and voices and guts over years of development. Sarah Sutherland, for all you gave to the play since before a single word was written—Rosemary will forever be filled with a you-ness. Isha Menon, Ella Caldwell and Casey Filips for stepping in and bringing words to life with skill and heart. A production team, who at the point of writing this I am only just getting to know, but am already in awe of: Sophie Woodward, Giovanna Yate Gonzalez, Danni Esposito, Max Bowyer, and Rain Okpamen. I know how lucky I am to get to work with all of you. Also: Mark Wilson for turning complex economic theory into graspable allegories about mug factories. Ibo Halacoglu, Allee Richards and Emily Sheehan for good notes. Bonnie, Sarah, Monica, and John for talking to me about your experiences of working in fast food kitchens. Eva Seymour, Belle Hansen, and Tilly Gibbs for the Sims chats. Chanella Macri, Harvey Zielinski, Dushan Philips, Kate Cole, Samuel Rowe, Maddie Nunn, Tahlee

Fereday, George Lingard, and Shaun Wykes for all you contributed to the play during developments. Fleur Kilpatrick, Bridget Mackey, you know. Alberto Di Troia and Vidya Rajan for readings and spot-on feedback in my very small living room. The beautiful people at Currency Press. Felisa, Deb, Frankie and Michael for pep talks, about anything, whenever I needed them. Michael also thank you for getting me that job at Pizza Hut when I was 20. Ella (again), Fiona and everyone at Red Stitch, thanks for fighting the art fight and letting me be a part of it. Pretty much nowhere else would let me do this play this way. Also thanks to my dog, Dragon, for sitting next to me while I work.

Morgan Rose
Playwright

DIRECTOR'S NOTE

Morgan and I first worked together in 2017, when I directed *desert, 6:29pm* for Red Stitch. That work saw Morgan begin to play with the devices that are at the core of *Fast Food*: fantasy, memory and hidden thoughts. In *Fast Food* Morgan wanted to take those ideas and tip the scales in fantasy's favour, so that we spend most of our time in the world of daydream and subconsciousness. What Morgan has done so well is keep us tethered to reality enough so that the fantasy never feels like it's for its own sake, but rather emerges from a need to escape—the past, the future, the relentless crush of capitalism, or ourselves.

Most of us lead lives that are outwardly small, but this doesn't mean that they are not dramatic or rich ozr complicated on the inside. Morgan's work insists that the small things are actually the big things and that which we imagine, and want, and call up inside ourselves is as real as the tangible 'reality' in front of us.

In some theatres I think there would be a temptation to stage this play in a way that involved a lot of radical design transformation, where you used big effects and visual tricks to move between worlds—but there's something about the intimacy and scale of Red Stitch that I think serves the play better. Being in a smaller venue where fine detail is so visible and where there is less emphasis on effects means that the line between reality and fantasy is finer, more permeable and the distance between the two places is not so great—they become concurrent, rather than neatly separated, which feels more truthful, at least in my experience.

A work like this would not be possible without the Red Stitch Ink program so thank you to Red Stitch for backing writers like Morgan to make work that is unconventional in form and structure.

Bridget Balodis
Director

MORGAN ROSE
PLAYWRIGHT

Morgan Rose was born in New Orleans, grew up in New Mexico, and currently lives in Melbourne. She is an internationally produced playwright, performance maker and dramaturg. Her work is contemporary and darkly funny, with an element of absurdism. In addition to her text-based work she has a background in physical theatre and devising. She has studied with SITI Company (NYC, USA), Pacific Performance Project (Seattle, USA), Zen Zen Zo Physical Theatre (Brisbane, Australia), and Dairakudakan (Hakuba, Japan). She completed a Master of Writing for Performance at VCA in 2013. In 2020 she was a dramaturgy placement with Malthouse Theatre as part of the Besen Family Artist Program. She was a recipient of the INK writing commission with Red Stitch Actors Theatre in 2014 and again in 2018. Recent works include: *Virgins and Cowboys* (writer, Theatreworks, Griffin Theatre), *Everyone Is Famous* (writer, Riot Stage/Speakeasy), *Lord Willing and the Creek Don't Rise* (writer, MKA/MTC NEON), *The BachelorS17E05* (co-creator, The People/La Mama), *desert, 6:29pm* (writer, Red Stitch/Wuzhen Festival/Currency Press), and *little girls alone in the woods* (Canberra Youth Theatre/Currency Press). She is resident writer at youth company Riot Stage (riotstage.com) and co-founder of the company The People (thepeoplemaketheatre.com). More info on her work at roseisnotarose.com. She is left handed.

BRIDGET BALODIS
DIRECTOR

Bridget Balodis is currently Director in Residence at Malthouse. For Malthouse she has directed *Stay Woke* by Aran Thangaratnam and the digital productions of *The Lockdown Monologues* and *Hello, World!* also at Malthouse Bridget was Assistant Director on the large-scale immersive work, *Because The Night*, Her other recent directing credits include *HYDRA* (Darebin Arts), *She is Vigilante* (Theatre Works), *MORAL PANIC* (Darebin Arts), *desert, 6:29pm* (Red Stitch Actors' Theatre/Wuhzen Theatre Festival), *GROUND CONTROL* (Next Wave/Brisbane Festival), *Jurassica* (Red Stitch Actors' Theatre/Critical Stages), and *Kids Killing Kids* (Next Wave). Bridget was Assistant Director on *The Dream* (Bell Shakespeare) and *The Histrionic* (Malthouse Theatre/Sydney Theatre Company). In 2015 and 2016 she lived in New York, where she worked with downtown legends Elevator Repair Service and for Wooster Group alumna Anna Kohler. She was a part of the inaugural Melbourne Theatre Company's Women Director's program in 2014 and has been the recipient of the Ian Potter Cultural Trust Award, Mike Walsh Fellowship, and Dame Joan Sutherland Award

SOPHIE WOODWARD
SET & COSTUME DESIGN

Sophie is a Melbourne-based set and costume designer. Sophie graduated with a Bachelor of Production (Design) from VCA in 2010 winning the Beleura John Tallis Design Award in her final year. Sophie recently designed *Iphigenia in Splott* and *Grace* at Red Stitch Actors Theatre and *Burn This* at FortyFive Downstairs. Earlier design work from Sophie includes *Hungry Ghosts* (MTC), *The One* and *Mr Burns, A Post Electric Play* (FortyFive Downstairs); *Those Who Fall in Love like Anchors Dropped Upon the Ocean Floor* , *Between the Clouds*, *Pyjama Girl* and *Letters from the Border* (Hothouse Theatre); *Extinction*, *Rules for Living*, *You got Older*, *Uncle Vanya*, *The Honey Bees*, *The Village Bike*, *Wet House*, *Love Love Love*, *4,000 Miles* and *Day One, A Hotel, Evening* (Red Stitch); *Thigh Gap*, *A Long Day's Dying*, *Conspiracy*, *Patient 12* and *The Savages of Wirramai* (LaMama); *Love Song* (Melbourne Fringe); and *The Sapphires*, *Glorious*, *Educating Rita*, *Shirley Valentine*, *Always Patsy Cline* and *All My Love*

(Hit Productions). Sophie was Design Assistant on *An Ideal Husband* and *Twelfth Night* (MTC). You can view Sophie's work at www.sophiewoodwarddesign.com

GIOVANNA YATE GONZALEZ
LIGHTING DESIGN

Giovanna Yate Gonzalez is a Colombian professional dancer who has expanded her skill set in Australia through the production bachelor at VCA in Lighting Design. She has participated in various performances in Australia, for example, as the lighting designer for the *The Book of Everything*, at Geelong Repertory Theatre Company in 2019, the interdisciplinary dance project *Ten Degrees* and the musical *Sweet Charity* in 2021 at VCA. Furthermore, *Trash Pop Butterflies*, *Dance Dance Dance Paradise* January 2022 at MKA– Midsumma Festival and *Nora: A Doll's House* at the Union House Theatre in April 2022. She had a collaborative lighting installation, *Talk to Me*, with musician Monica Lim at the Bundoora Homestead Art Centre.

DANNI ESPOSITO
SOUND DESIGN & COMPOSITION

Danni is a gender-queer sound designer and composer from Naarm/Melbourne. They specialise in sound design and composition for theatre, immersive works and film. Danni's most notable credits include sound design and composition for Malthouse Theatre's 2020 season launch; *Hydra* (Double Water Sign Theatre); *SLUTNIK* (Midsumma Festival); *Guerilla Sabbath* (Midsumma Festival); *Cactus* (La Mama Theatre); *Punk Rock* (Patalog Theatre); *Slut* (The Burrow); *The Dream Laboratory* (Essential Theatre); *Treats* (Fever103 Theatre); *Land* (Three Fates Theatre Company); *Never Said Motel* (Writers Festival, OK Motels); *Adam* (Midsumma Festival); *Tram Lights Up* (Bighouse Arts);

Western Edge Youth Arts (WEYA–In School, Artist In Residency). Danni is a design graduate of the Victorian College of the Arts (VCA), holding a Bachelor of Fine Arts (Production). Danni is a proud alumni of MTC's industry-leading Women in Theatre program. Danni is a current panel member of the Green Room Theatre Companies Panel for 2022.

KATIE SFETKIDIS
LIGHTING DESIGN MENTOR

Katie Sfetkidis is a lighting designer and contemporary artist based in Naarm. She has worked extensively in theatre, dance and experimental performance across Australia and internationally. Credits include: Melbourne Theatre Company (*Touching the Void*; *Abigail's Party*), Malthouse Theatre (*SS Metaphor*; *Chase*; *Meme Girls*), Belvoir Theatre (*Kill the Messenger*), Red Stitch Actors Theatre (*The Moor*; *Suddenly Last Summer*), Joel Bray Dance (*Considerable Sexual License*; *Daddy*), Little Ones Theatre (*Merciless Gods*; *Pyscho Beach Party*) and Aphids (*Easy Rider*; *Exit Strategies*; *The Director*). In 2015 Katie won a Green Room Award for her lighting design for *Meme Girls* and has been nominated many times. Currently Katie is the co-deputy chair of the Green Room Awards Panel for Mainstage Companies and a committee member for the Victorian Branch of the Australian Production Design Guild.

TOM HEALY
DRAMATURG

Tom graduated from the Victorian College of the Arts in 1989. Over the past 30 years he has worked as a director, dramaturg and actor for theatre companies around the nation. His previous productions include: *American Song* (national tour), *Jumpers for Goalposts* and *The Shape of Things* (national tour, Red Stitch

Actors' Theatre); *Heisenberg* (MTC); *The Kid* (Griffin); *The Spook* (Malthouse Theatre); *Elegy, The Sign of the Seahorse, Ancient Enmity, Insouciance, The Fat Boy* and *Falling Petals* (Playbox); *Let's Get it On* (Room 8); *Doris Day—So Much More Than the Girl Next Door* (Boldjack); *Disarming Rosetta* and *Inside Out* (Hothouse Theatre); *Good Evening* (Token) with Sean Micallef and Stephen Curry; *The Man In Black* (Folsom Prison Productions); Eddie Perfect's solo shows, *Drink Pepsi, Bitch!* (Malthouse Theatre and tour); and *Angry Eddie* (Chapel Off Chapel). Tom is currently the Associate Dramaturg at Red Stitch. Previous positions include Head of Acting and Directing at Flinders Drama Centre, Literary Manager at the Australian Script Centre, Artistic Director of the Australian National Playwrights' Conference and Artistic Associate at Playbox. He has been a proud member of the MEAA since 1989.

RAIN OKPAMEN
STAGE MANAGER

Rain is a freelance stage manager and production manager. Since 2019 she's been working in Melbourne's independent theatre scene. Her stage manager credits include; Goodfellow Theatre Company's production of *A Midsummer Night's Dream* directed by Jesse Novella; *Scarborough* directed by Bronwen Coleman; Encore Theatre Company's production of *The Witches* directed by David Collins; TBC Theatre's production of *Rust* directed by Renee Palmer, Alice Darling and Trudi Boatwright and played as part of the 2020 Midsumma Festival; Red Stitch Theatre's production of *Single Ladies* directed by Bagryana Popov and *The Cane* directed by Kirsten Von Bibra; Anthropocene Play Company play reading of *Ignis* directed by Bronwen Coleman; Thomas Carr College production of *Matilda the Musical*; and *The Darkening Sky* at TheatreWorks written and directed by Richard Murphet. She was production manager for *Security* directed by Alice

Qin; and for St Martin's production of *Gene Tree* directed by Nadja Kostich; lighting operator at Watch This's production of *Into The Woods* directed by Sonya Suares and Mel Hillman; stage manager at the 2022 development of *Zaffé* directed by Stephanie Ghajar; replacement stage manager at Red Stitch Theatre' production of *Grace* directed by Sarah Goodes; and Melbourne Theatre Company's development of *Only Players* written and directed by David Williams.

MAX BOWYER
ASSISTANT SET & COSTUME DESIGNER / ASSISTANT STAGE MANAGER

Max is an English-born set, costume and digital designer/maker and technician, based in Melbourne/Naarm. Graduating from The Victorian College of the Arts (Production) in 2021, Max's passion for live performance design stems from its power to connect modern audiences to important stories and messages. His credits include set design for *Cloud 9* (VCA), *The Execution Will Not Be Televised* (Impending Storm Productions), *Baccarat* (The German Romantics) and *Legally Blonde* (UMMTA), with assistant design credits for *Das Rheingold* (Melbourne Opera Company). His construction credits include *And She Would Stand Like This* (Antipodes Theatre Co), *The Cane* (Red Stitch), *Enlightenment* (Elbow Room Theatre), *Our House* (VCA), and *Mad Forest* (VCA). Max is excited to be taking on this new role within the Fast Food team.

KEVIN HOJERSLEV
ASSISTANT DIRECTOR

Kevin Hojerslev is writer, performer and dramaturg who focuses on the creation and development of new work. He is especially interested in evolving the architecture and conventions of scripts to better suit contemporary theatremaking styles and emergent performances, particularly with regards to how script formats can be more supportive of group devised projects and other writing processes that do not come from singular authors. He is also drawn to theatre as a platform for creating collective imagined futures for communities. He sees the democratic and live aspects of theatre and theatre making as an effective vehicle for harnessing the imaginations of audiences towards considering personal and shared futures. Kevin was born in Bangkok and has lived his life across Australia, China and Thailand. Making and watching theatre across multiple countries while being immersed in their culture for long periods of time has given him a nuanced and sensitive appreciation of how art emerges from culture and how culture shapes around art. Returning to Melbourne in 2018, Kevin began his undergraduate studies at the VCA, completing their Theatre course in 2021. It was here that Kevin gained an appreciation for the diversity of theatre making processes.

CASEY FILIPS
LEONARD

Casey is a Greek-Australian actor/writer/comedian from Melbourne, Australia. Upon graduating from his degree at the National Theatre Drama School in 2017, Casey was selected as the prestigious Red Stitch Graduate Ensemble Member for 2018. His credits include *The Antipodes* (Red Stitch), *desert, 6:29pm* (Red Stitch/Wuzhen International Theatre Fest), *Dance Nation* (Red Stitch), *Some Happy Day* (Soup Kitchen Productions), *Hello, World!* (Malthouse Theatre), and *Hydra* (Darebin Speakeasy). In 2019 Casey also traveled to Paris, France to study at the internationally renowned Ecole Philippe Gaulier (Theatre School), where he was mentored by theatre and comedy royalty Philippe Gaulier. Casey is also a comedian and writer, performing stand-up across Melbourne with the likes of Dave Thornton, Nick Capper, and many more. Casey is thrilled to be back at Red Stitch treading the boards with such an amazing creative team and thanks you for supporting live theatre.

KEVIN HOFBAUER
TROY

Kevin is an Australian actor who has worked consistently in TV and theatre since graduating from VCA, debuting with the role of Constable Christian Tapu in the hit police drama *Rush*. His most recent on-screen performances were in Paramount's *Spreadsheet* and Netflix's *Clickbait*. He has also appeared in *Playing for Keeps, Informer 3838, Neighbours, True Stories with Hamish & Andy, Sisters, Offspring, Mr. & Mrs. Murder* and *Small Time Gangster*. Kevin's MTC credits include *Touching the Void*, directed by Petra Kalive, *Macbeth*, directed by Simon Phillips and *Menagerie*; *Trevor* and *The Flick* for Red Stitch and *Tame* for The Malthouse Theatre.

ISHA MENON
G.

Originally from Canberra and of Indian and Dutch heritage, Isha is a curious and adventurous performer who graduated from the Victorian College of the Arts in 2021 with a Bachelor in Theatre. Isha thoroughly enjoys working in both comedy and melodrama as a performer and as a writer/theatremaker. In 2019, she wrote, directed and performed in a two hander *girl walks home from a train* as part of the inaugural student-lead arts festival *Discord* held at the Victorian College of the Arts (VCA). In 2021 she performed *Very Nice Pot Plants* (dir. Karla Livingston and Zachary Sheridan) at Theatreworks Glasshouse venue. Some of her credits from her time at VCA include being part of *Otello: What's Changed* (dir. Draf Draffin), where she wrote and performed *Butterfly!*, and *Sleep Faster Show Cat* (dir. Emma Hall), a semi-improvised endurance theatre piece set entirely in the surreal online world of Zoom.

CHI NGUYEN
RIVER

Chi was born and raised in Vietnam and moved to Australia when she was 16 to pursue the performing arts. Chi is a graduate of The Victorian College of the Arts (VCA) where she received the Grace Marion Wilson Scholarship for Excellence in Acting. Chi's recent TV credits are recurring role of Megan Vu in Amazon Prime's original series *Class Of '07*, Jeanette Dao in Amazon Prime's original series *The Wilds*, and Juliana in ABC's *FISK*, in which Chi performed and co-wrote two episodes with Kitty Flanagan. Chi also starred in Vietnamese-Australian comedy web series *Phi and Me* and played Au Pair in Victoria Thane's web series *Sonia and Cherry*. 2022 will see Chi perform in *LAURINDA* (dir. Petra Kalive), making it her Melbourne Theatre Company debut. In 2019, Chi wrote and performed a season of her debut solo comedy cabaret *LOTUS* (Nominated Best Cabaret at Melbourne Fringe 2019). Other theatrical credits include Tam (lead) in The Shift Theatre's *Hallowed Ground: Women Doctors In War* (toured with Regional Arts Victoria and internationally to Edinburgh Fringe 2019), Lead Player in Arena Theatre Company's *AIR RACE* (dir. Christian Leavesley) and Mother Courage in VCA's *Mother Courage and Her Children* (dir. Chris Kohn).

ELLA CALDWELL
ROSEMARY

Ella is a founding member of Red Stitch and has been Artistic Director of the company since July 2013. During this time, Ella has evolved and steered the company's new writing program, INK, providing significant opportunities for the development and production of new writing at Red Stitch. Since its inception, this program has produced numerous acclaimed productions and toured nationally and internationally. Most recently, Ella directed the critically acclaimed Australian premiere season of Ella Hickson's epic work, *Oil*. In 2018 Ella directed the acclaimed Australian premiere season of *The Antipodes* by Annie Baker. Previous directorial work includes the sold-out Victorian premiere season of Joanna Murray-Smith's *Fury* and the Australian premiere production of *Incognito* by Nick Payne, both directed in collaboration with ensemble member Brett Cousins, and the world premiere of Caleb Lewis's *The Honeybees*. As an actor, Ella most recently performed in the world premiere of *desert, 6:29pm* by Morgan Rose, directed by Bridget Balodis. Following a premiere season at Red Stitch, *desert, 6:29pm* sold out at Wuzhen Theatre Festival in China on the company's first international tour.

RED STITCH ACTORS' THEATRE

We are an actor-led ensemble, enriching our community by empowering artists as cultural leaders. We inspire audiences with compelling contemporary theatre that engages with the complexities of humanity and reveals us to ourselves. Our organisational model nurtures artistic vibrancy and growth.

Red Stitch is a creative hub, offering scope for artists to make work they are passionate about in a sector where such opportunities are limited. As the ensemble and executives of Red Stitch, we provide a platform where leading practitioners can hone their craft and take risks, and emerging artists can work alongside mid-career and seasoned professionals. We play a vital role in the development and presentation of new Australian works through our INK playwriting program, promoting local voices alongside acclaimed contemporary international work which may not otherwise be seen by local audiences.

www.redstitch.net

Red Stitch would like to thank the following supporters who generously contribute to our INK program.

Australian Government
RISE Fund

CREATIVE VICTORIA

CITY OF PORT PHILLIP

Cybec Foundation

MALCOLM ROBERTSON FOUNDATION

THE PORTLAND HOUSE FOUNDATION

THE ROBERT SALZER FOUNDATION

PLAYKING FOUNDATION

Lyngala Foundation

THE MYER FOUNDATION

SIDNEY MYER FUND

Kindred

www.ingramcontent.com/pod-product-compliance
Lightning Source LLC
Chambersburg PA
CBHW050018090426
42734CB00021B/3323